Gut Intelligence: ALIGN

Gut Intelligence: ALIGN

TESTIMONIALS

"ALIGN is a gift for anyone that seeks transformation, personally or professionally. The knowledge and techniques Susan shares will empower you to step into your greatest potential and live an authentic, joyful and abundant life."

-Jennifer Schiellack, Director
PwC

"The book is filled with stories and skills on how to live a lighter life aligned to your dreams. I highly recommend it to anyone wanting to reach their potential."

-Charlie Berens, Comedian
Manitowoc Minute

"With Gut Intelligence Susan has added a new practical dimension to staying true to my personal and professional vision, values and goals. This is a paradigm shift in thinking, feeling and doing. Susan can do it for you too!"

-Gayle P. Russel, PhD, RN

"Susan's book provides practical tips for creating and maintaining personal and professional focus, purpose and alignment toward achieving your goals.

-Christine Steeno, Sr. Vice President
Willis Towers Watson

"Susan is one of the most consistent coaches in the industry, year after year after year. She masterfully brings new exercises again and again to help us all transform our thinking. This time her specific work on slowing down and getting beyond the chatterbox in our minds is priceless!"

-Rick Schaefer, MD
Author of Extreme Thought Makeover

"Susan Wehrley quantifies the skills that we need to ensure we are making wise decisions—both in our personal and professional lives. In the staffing business, we deal with people who have the three brains. Her book will help us to understand our candidates as well as ourselves."

-Carol Ann Schneider, CPC, SPHR - Chief Executive Officer
SEEK Career/Staffing

"I felt like Susan's book was written for me. It motivated me to change my life and align to my vision, values and goals!"

-Debbie Rollick, Client Partner
FranklinCovey Education

Be Your Best Self As You Reach Your Vision, Values & Goals

SUSAN K. WEHRLEY

Copyright © 2017 by Susan K. Wehrley

All rights reserved. No part of this book may be used or reproduced in any manner whatsoever without the written permission of the author, Susan K. Wehrley, except in the case of brief quotations embodied in critical articles or reviews. All photos used with permission and/or credit given.

Published by Thomas & Kay, LLC
Milwaukee, WI

Editing: Lesley DeMartini

Cartoons by Tim Decker

Photography by Cindy Lance

Printed by Create Space in the United States of American

10 9 8 7 6 5 4 3 2 1

Library of Congress Cataloging-in Publication Data is available for this title.

ISBN-10: 0972950540

ISBN-13: 978-0-9729505-4-1

Contact:
Email: Info@BIZremedies.com
Websites: www.BIZremedies.com & www.GutIntelliigence.com

To all my clients over the last 30 years-
Thank you for your business, what you taught me and how you allowed me into your organizations and lives. Because of you I am truly blessed!

Gut Intelligence: ALIGN

TABLE OF CONTENTS

SECTION I
ALIGN the Unconscious Knowing of your GUT and Desire of Your HEART, with the Conscious Wisdom of Your MIND—to Reach Your Vision, Values and Goals with Greater Mindfulness..2

- How Gut Intelligence Can Align You to Your Vision, Values and Goals..4
- The Power of Breathing, Curiosity & Detachment............17
- Increasing Your Gut Alert and Navigation Skills................21
- The Gut Intelligence MEDITATION 26
- How to Increase Your Locus of Control and Align to Your Vision, Values and Goals..30
- Don't Depend on Your Happenings for Your Happiness...43
- Practice Gut Intelligence to increase Discernment and Decrease Dis-ease...47

SECTION II:
8 Spiritual Principles to Help You Align to Your Vision, Values and Goals....53

Overview: Becoming Your Best Self on Your Journey to Your Vision, Values and Goals!....................................55

- **ALIGN Principle 1: Be Humble:** 61
  The Gateway to Your Connection and Calling
- **ALIGN Principle 2: Ask, Believe and Receive:** 66
  Creating an Honest Relationship with Self and Others
- **ALIGN Principle 3: Forgive, Let Go and Learn.** 71
  Unconscious Beliefs and Biases Inhibit Our Ability to Surrender
- **ALIGN Principle 4: Stay Open-minded and Get Curious:** 76
  Curiosity Bridges the Gap of Differences
- **ALIGN Principle 5: Practice Gratitude:** 81
  Detaching from Outcomes and Preconceived Notions
- **ALIGN Principle 6: Grace and Synchronicity:** 87
  Stepping in the Unknown
- **ALIGN Principle 7: Focus on Your Vision and Desire** 92
  Feel how great it will be when you arrive!
- **ALIGN Principle 8: Access Your Power** 97
  Slowing it down to align

SECTION III Daily Lessons, Affirmations and Challenges to Help You Stay Aligned: 103

ALIGN Principle 1: BE HUMBLE Days 1-5 105
- Day 1: You are but a thread among the fabric
- Day 2: Accept yourself unconditionally, including your shortcomings
- Day 3: Believe in something bigger than you
- Day 4: Engage others
- Day 5: Appreciate contribution

ALIGN Principle 2: ASK, BELIEVE AND RECEIVE Days 1-5 117
- Day 1: Ask for assistance
- Day 2: Focus on believing
- Day 3: Believe in your worth
- Day 4: Focus on receiving by eliminating stinkin-thinkin
- Day 5: Set a vision to receive help

ALIGN Principle 3: FORGIVE, LET GO AND LEARN Days 1-5 129
- Day 1: Change your mindset: It's all perfect!

- Day 2: Forgive yourself, instead of projecting your disappointment on others
- Day 3: Let go of expectations from others, but not your dreams
- Day 4: Learn where you are playing the victim, therefore giving your power away
- Day 5: Take responsibility for creating what you want

ALIGN PRIPLE 4: STAY OPEN-MINDED AND GET CURIOUS............141
- Day 1: You have plenty of time, so stop rushing
- Day 2: The difference between the chatter box and the still small voice
- Day 3: Eliminate fear by connecting to your Gut Intelligence
- Day 4: Trust your Gut Intelligence even it feels uncomfortable
- Day 5: Stay in the mindset of wonder

ALIGN Principle 5: PRACTICE GRATITUDE……………………………………..153
- Day 1: Detach from the outcomes
- Day 2: Breathe past fear and connect with gratitude
- Day 3: Change your schema
- Day 4: Learn to compliment others
- Day 5: Be grateful for your uniqueness

ALIGN PRINCIPLE 6: EMBRACE SYNCHRONICITY…………………………..165
- Day 1: Step into the unknown
- Day 2: Let go of your need to control
- Day 3: Create your thoughts
- Day 4: Waiting in the unknown build's discernment
- Day 5: Follow-through with your part of the partnership

ALIGN PRINCIPLE 7: FOCUS ON YOUR VISION & DESIRE……………….177
- Day 1: Focus on what you want, not what you don't want
- Day 2: Learn how your pain is prompting your purpose
- Day 3: How your passion leads you to your purpose
- Day 4: Learn how to stay connected to your WHY, so drama doesn't get you off track

- Day 5: Don't get caught in the comparison trap that steals your passion

ALIGN Principle 8: ACCESS YOUR POWER..................................189
- Day 1: You are bigger than all that "stuff"
- Day 2: Ask-lead yourself to a connection with your power
- Day 3: Be unafraid in the face of adversity and criticism
- Day 4: Stay firm and true to yourself
- Day 5: Keep a level head of self-assurance

SECTION IV Self-Assessment...201
- **Gut Intelligence Assessment**..203
- **8 Spiritual Principles Assessment**....................................205
- **Summary Discussion**...209

ACKNOWLEDGEMENTS

To my clients over the last 30 years who allowed me into their businesses and lives—thank you for trusting your businesses and employees with me and my techniques. I am truly honored.

To my daughters Lisa Wiltz and Alex Wehrley—thank you for the countless encouragement, support and input on the book. It is so fun to see how talented you both have become. Lisa—your attention to detail and marketing viewpoint is amazing. Alex-you really are supportive and get exactly what it is I do and how to message it to the world in a way that is appealing.

To Lesley DeMartini—as with the first Gut Intelligence book—you did a great job editing the book and giving honest feedback on where things needed to be clearer! You are talented and so enjoyable to work with!

To Cindy Lance—you have a natural talent when it comes to photography! I love the photos on the cover and back cover you took, as well as the many photos that are on the website because of you! Thank you for your contribution and your sisterhood.

And finally, and surely not lastly—Tim Decker the cartoonist. Thank you for giving life to Rosemary and Fred, the two characters in the book. All things happen for a reason and your caricature gave them the personality the book needed to inspire us all. Thank you for your talent and friendship.

And, I would be remiss if I did not thank God and the Holy Spirit who inspired me to do this book. May you all be blessed!

Gut Intelligence: ALIGN

NOTE TO THE READER
From Susan K. Wehrley

Susan K. Wehrley is the author of eight books. She has been a coach and consultant for 30 years helping corporations business owners, executives, and growth-minded individuals reach their full potential.

Learn more about Susan and her work at www.BIZremedies.com

Last year, I wrote my first book on Gut Intelligence. I'm not going to lie: I expected it to be an overnight success and best seller. It wasn't, and here I am one year later writing my second book on Gut Intelligence called Gut Intelligence: ALIGN.

You may wonder why I am continuing to write on this topic. Well, besides the fact that the trademark company insisted I write another book on Gut Intelligence within this timeframe, it is because I am committed to teach this skill. In Gut Intelligence: ALIGN, you will find it to be less academic, proving how Gut Intelligence is scientifically proven, and more about applying it to your life, so you can be your best self as you reach your vision, values and goals. Not only will you get practical tips on how to align your gut, heart and mind for better decision-making, you will get 8 Spiritual Principles to help you be your best self as you achieve new levels of success.

Many warned me about calling these principles "Spiritual Principles". Their concern was it may alienate business from using my services and hiring me for Organizational alignment. I do understand the separation of church and state and considered this truth in the past. But as I have become more aligned with my vision, values and goals—it was no longer possible to leave out my own truth in a book about being your best self as you reach your vision, values and goals.

In my experience, when we have increased Gut Intelligence, we are living a life in Intuitive Alignment. This means we are no longer listening to our ego-voice, but instead our spirit-voice within. We are not only integrating our Gut, Heart and Mind in decision-making—we are also inviting the Holy Spirit in on the conversation.

Businesses may or may not be ready to hear my message. The beautiful thing is: I am speaking my truth anyway. By letting go of the outcome and being in full alignment with who I am and what I feel called to do, I am hopefully not just writing this book—I am being the book by showing you an example of ALIGN

Unlike the first Gut Intelligence book, this is a book where we meet two characters who represent aspects of our self. One is Rosemary, who struggles with typical female gender biases and beliefs: She believes she has to be all-giving and supportive of others to get the love and approval she otherwise could just give herself.

Then there is Fred. Like many men, Fred has reduced himself to a provider who is obligated to take care of the family by giving up his own passion and purpose. Money becomes his focus and he becomes very reactive when he doesn't get the outcome he desires.

Both Rosemary and Fred learn the skills from the book to be their best self as they reach their vision, values and goals. This includes both of them consciously defining them so they can make conscious decisions to reach that which they say they desire. Not only will you identify and be inspired by Rosemary's and Fred's transformation, you will receive practical tools and tips to transform into your best self as well.

My dream is every business owner, leaders, executive, and growth-minded man and woman will purchase Gut Intelligence: ALIGN so we can live in a better world, surrounded by people who consciously choose who they will be in the moments that otherwise would be testy or turbulent.

May this book bless you and help you to be all you were meant to be as you reach new heights toward your vision, values and goals!

Blessings-

Susan K. Wehrley, author

SECTION I

ALIGN

The Unconscious Knowing of Your GUT

And Desire of Your HEART

With the Conscious Wisdom of Your MIND

To Reach Your Vision, Values and Goals with Greater Mindfulness.

How Gut Intelligence Can Align You to Your Vision, Values and Goals

You deserve happiness.

And you deserve love.

You also deserve to realize the life you want to live—free from pain and full of safety, security and fulfillment.

But often we live like my clients Fred and Rosemary—a business owner and a senior executive—who don't take the time to figure out what their vision is, in business or in life. In fact, like most of us, Fred and Rosemary often run so hard to try to meet their daily expectations that they don't really know what it would look or feel like if they were living to their full potential and not striving so hard.

While most of us know that a vision is an aspiration or direction we want to accomplish, most of us fall short of aligning our moment-to-moment decisions for the future outcomes we say we want. When we are unaware of what decisions would align to our vision, we often give in to instant gratification—satisfying the urges of our lesser self—rather than foregoing our gratification in the present moment. Other times, we are just striving hard to reach daily and weekly expectations without understanding the ultimate "why" of we are doing all we are doing—besides just paying the bills. This endless cycle occurs because we are trying to find some means of self-satisfaction and buy-in to the promises of "more" as the better life.

One would think a senior executive like Rosemary would find it easy to define a vision for herself, both personally and professionally. But like most people, Rosemary has lost touch with her inner knowing: the inner compass that could guide her in discerning how to meet all the demands around her. Instead, Rosemary believes she must work hard to prove herself as an executive because she is one of the only women on the senior management team. Part of her strategy in proving herself is to be a team player, which she views as being available, saying "yes," and working long hours.

What blocks Rosemary, a single, career-minded woman, from getting what she really wants out of life—a fulfilling career and an emotionally connected love life—is her own inability to align her gut, heart and head to fully guide her in every moment.

While Rosemary has a vision and is conscious of her values for love and success, she lacks other guiding principles, standards of behavior and morale codes to ensure she is aligning each decision to what she wants most. Values help guide us on how we will behave as we move towards what we want to achieve.

Fred, who is married and owns several retail establishments around the country, struggles with aligning his values in his everyday behavior. A plaque in his conference room indicates he values both growth and collaboration. However, when push comes to shove, Fred resorts to top-down communication when his revenue does not exceed his expenses. This is why simply etching our values on a plaque is not effective. It gives no meaning to the hierarchy of values or the storyline of our commitment to respond in various situations.

Fred and Rosemary, while both struggling with different reactions to varying circumstances, are both being governed by unconscious gender biases and beliefs. For women, these tendencies include a belief that they must be all-giving, self-sacrificial and accommodating to be of worth. For men, it is the belief that "if it's meant to be, it's up to me!" While not all women and men think only in these unconscious gender beliefs, it is important to understand just how you have been affected and, therefore, may unconsciously react.

Rosemary, for example, would tell you she struggles with the amount of time she perceives is required in order to have the thriving career she wants along with the demanding love life she imagines. She never feels like she is enough to "have it all" or find the balance in her life she desires. While she would blame "demands and lack of time" as the reasons, the real root cause for Rosemary's self-doubt is her unconscious belief that she cannot have it all. This unconscious belief blocks her from her Gut Intelligence that would otherwise give her discernment in choosing supportive relationships, setting boundaries and collaborating on who might do what.

For Fred, he struggles with letting go and trusting others to adequately run his business. While his mind and heart tell him that collaboration makes sense, he overreacts when his gut gets alerted to undesirable results—unconsciously believing, "If it's meant to be, it's up to me!" Like many men, this was instilled at a young age when he was told to "not cry," "buck it up," "make it happen" and that "your worth is your pocketbook." In Fred's case, this was amplified in his mid-twenties when his father had a heart attack and he was told he must take over his dad's business and figure it out—that the family was counting on him!

While Rosemary and Fred would tell you they both envision letting go more, neither of them knows exactly how to do that in a way that they can still achieve results. Both Rosemary and Fred, like many of us, lack the wisdom to know the truth and the guts to do something about it in the moment that matters. This skill is called Gut Intelligence.

Gut Intelligence is the ability to acknowledge what we know unconsciously in our GUT and desire in our HEART in order to allow our MIND to put the pieces of the puzzle together and consciously align our decisions to what we envision and value most.

Gut Intelligence allows us to yield to instant gratification, so we can align to longer-lasting results. This means that instead of jumping in to fix a situation or person, or fleeing from a conversation to avoid conflict, we would step in to affect the change we envision in others.

The ability to align our gut, heart and mind requires an acknowledgement of each of their separate functions and how they operate in order to achieve Gut Intelligence.

The Gut Intelligence Functions are as follows:
- The *Gut* alerts us to cues at the tip of the iceberg.
- The *Heart* reminds us what we value most.
- The *Mind* puts the pieces of the puzzle together so the unconscious knowing of our gut and heart becomes conscious. This allows us to align our gut and heart together to discover possibilities we otherwise would not see if we reacted from our unconscious biases and beliefs.

Like so many of us, both Rosemary and Fred work hard to reach their goals. However, because they both have not fully explored their own unconscious or conscious beliefs and desires, they often react out of alignment with their best selves—and their vision, values and goals.

Throughout this book, you will see how Rosemary and Fred become more conscious as they aspire to be their best selves and realize their vision, values and goals in a more loving and joyful way. Instead of just checking off their to do lists and moving unconsciously through their daily activities, Rosemary and Fred learn to listen to the wisdom of their gut, heart and head so they are in alignment with what they want to become.

You will witness, through the lives of Rosemary and Fred, how Gut Intelligence can assist you in making decisions strategically and spontaneously. This means not only will you learn ways to map out your vision, but you will also learn ways to re-establish your alignment when you face difficult people and situations. Increasing Gut Intelligence is especially helpful when facing unexpected twists and turns in the road so that we can respond consciously and make effective decisions.

What happens when we don't increase our Gut Intelligence and we only map out our plan? We often miss the cues at the tip of the iceberg that tell us a detour is ahead. As a result, we often say we felt blindsided—when the truth is, the signs were always there. We just didn't see them because we were too affixed to our plan.

We saw this a lot with companies affected by the economic downturn in 2007. Popular indicators such as the inflation rate, earnings growth, housing market, stock market, unemployment rate and short-term bills tell us if a recession is coming. When businesses don't use their Gut Intelligence to notice these cues at the tip of the iceberg and make adjustments in their strategic plans, they lose out.

Closer to the vest are a company's own internal indicators: revenue, profit margins, turnover, competition, marketplace trends and vendor changes. All of these give us "gut alerts" so we know when to pay attention and adjust. On the personal side of life, we see indicators in our relationships all the time, telling us if they are "just not that into you!"

When we listen to our Gut Intelligence, we can navigate these indicators early on and, therefore, stay aligned to our vision, values and goals in an ever-evolving world.

When we don't check in with this navigation center I call Gut Intelligence, we get "dis-ease." Dis-ease, gone unchecked, can turn into physical disease, mental disease or addictive behaviors. These more obvious conditions are simply indicators that we are no longer in alignment with our true self.

It's not as easy as it seems to define your vision for your life. Sometimes we know what it is we want, but we believe we don't deserve our heart's desire or believe what we want is possible. This causes us to deny or suppress our Gut Intelligence, which is the map to get us there. When we don't listen to this prompting and we take the easy path instead, we live in fear and self-doubt instead of courage and enlightenment.

Other times, we have no idea what we want. If this is the case, we often get stuck in people-pleasing or look for hints of what our life could be by looking at others' lives. We set our standards by looking to Facebook, advertising, our neighbors, churches, communities or our parents for the blueprint. Instead of looking inward for the answers, we look outward for examples of a "good life." The problem in looking outside ourselves for examples of a good life is that we don't get the good life that will satisfy the desires of our heart.

By looking outward, you see typical and expected ways for people to live. That is why so many people get in the cycle of going to college, getting married in their mid-twenties, buying a house, climbing the corporate ladder, having kids and working hard—only to end up divorce because this wasn't their vision or value deep down. I am certainly not pointing fingers, since this was my life in my 20s and 30s—I followed the social trend and fell into a traditional married lifestyle at a young age. It was wasn't until I got into my 50s that I realized marriage in and of itself offered me no security or love. What I wanted more than tradition was a connected, compatible, collaborative and committed relationship.

Unfortunately, it often takes a catalyst like divorce, death, getting dismissed from a job or a destructive behavior pattern for us to get honest with ourselves. When we finally get conscious enough, we can ask that aching pit in our stomach this question:

"How might I live a life fully aligned to my vision and values?"

Increased Gut Intelligence will help us align to the answer that is just right for us.

How does Gut Intelligence help us align decisions to our best self and reach for our vision, values and goals? Neuroscientist Urs Meyer from Zurich, Switzerland identified how our gut sends messages to our heart and brain through the vagus nerve. The vagus nerve reaches from the gut, touches the heart and extends to the brain—sending 100 million neurons and major neurotransmitters like serotonin, dopamine, glutamate, norepinephrine and nitric oxide to the heart and head-brain from our gut. This explains why we have a visceral reaction when something feels right or something feels off. The study indicates that the vagus nerve provides a feedback loop so our gut, heart and head-brain can communicate to one another. When we practice tapping into this navigation system, we become astute at discerning its messages to us.

For example, when our gut-brain has been alerted, we first are triggered in a fight/flight response because the amygdala in our brain gets activated. This tells us to be on alert! Unfortunately, most people, like Fred, react to this strong visceral signal and jump into a fight or flight decision, which is always less than ideal.

In order to make the most effective decisions to align to our vision, values and goals, we must breathe into our gut and not react when alerted. Breathing into our gut increases Gut Intelligence and our decision-making ability. By slowing down our brainwaves, opening the corpus callosum, and getting past the amygdala, we can access the higher parts of the left and right hemispheres of our brain to avoid this fight/flight reaction and respond mindfully instead. This is the skill Fred is working on so he can become a more mindful leader.

Fred is beginning to understand that once he sends these unconscious neurotransmitters and neurons up the vagus nerve to his heart, he can first align to what he desires most before making a decision. We can all do this by asking ourselves this curious question:

"What do I really want most in this situation?"

Once we are reminded of our values and heart's desire, we can get curious and ask ourselves:

> *"Now, considering my heart's desire,*
> *How might I align my decision to what I want most?"*

This question will engage our brain's ability to integrate all the unconscious knowledge of the gut and use the language, logic and problem-solving skills of the head-brain to put the pieces of the puzzle together. This allows us to increase our Gut Intelligence and effectively align our best self to our vision, values and goals.

When you gain this alignment, instead of being confused, frazzled and doubtful—you become clear, calm and confident! You know you have arrived at your best solution because you have that "a-ha" knowing—a heightened awareness that sends chills down your body and makes the light bulb in your head switch on.

For Rosemary, strengthening her ability to listen to how her gut sends an alert at the tip of the iceberg (instead of going into self-doubt) is especially important. She tends to believe she is being over-sensitive because that's what she heard time and time again when others denied her insights. This kept her from fully achieving her Gut Intelligence and listening to the unconscious wisdom of her gut and heart that wanted to alert her to pay attention and remind her of what she wanted most. Instead, her self-doubt acted as a detour, making her believe she couldn't trust herself to clarify what decisions she needed to make to align to her vision, values and goals.

Once Rosemary and Fred learned the **3-Step Gut Intelligence ALIGN Practice,** both were more able to stay aligned to their vision, values and goals in the moments of choice that mattered most.

3-Step Gut Intelligence ALIGN Practice:
Step 1: Gut Alert (Pay attention to the sensations in your gut)
Do this by wondering, *"What is this feeling trying to tell me?"*
Step 2: Heart Alignment (Pay attention to the sensations in your heart)
Do this by wondering, *"What do I really want most of all in this situation?"*
Step 3: Mind Strategy (Pay attention to the facts)
Do this by wondering, *"How might I align to my vision, values and goals, given these facts?"*

Both Rosemary and Fred were advised to remember that the gut is simply an alert center. To increase our Gut Intelligence, we must integrate the heart and head in decision-making. This increases our Gut Intelligence so we can fully align to our vision, values and goals in the moments of choice.

The Power of Breathing, Curiosity & Detachment

We have all had the experience where our gut said one thing, our heart wanted another and our head was cloudy on what to do about this incongruence. This is because we saw cues at the tip of the iceberg that alerted us to something or someone not being in alignment with our vision, values and goals. Worst yet, we were attached to wanting to see it a certain way, so we denied what we knew.

Perhaps you've had a situation like Rosemary, where you were so physically attracted to a person that you tended to only see the things you shared in common in the beginning of the relationship. This satisfied your ego that desired an answer now: You finally found that person who satisfied your vision! Then, after a year or so, you saw behaviors that did not align to how this person represented him/herself earlier, and this relationship no longer aligned to your values. Your gut alerted you to this incongruence, but your heart was already attached to this person. Because you were not certain you could navigate this reality, you acted as though you didn't know what to do—but you really did!

Because you are not practicing the 3-Step Gut Intelligence Align Practice, you are stuck in the fight/flight part of your brain. Neither fleeing from the relationship nor fighting to create changes appeals to you. But what else can you do?

You can increase your Gut Intelligence by breathing more deeply, becoming more curious, and detaching from the outcome. When you do this, you can ask yourself:

"How might I stay aligned to my vision, values and goals, Considering this new information?"

By asking yourself this question, you will realize possibilities to stay aligned to yourself and not abandon your vision, values and goals.

Once Rosemary began practicing the 3-Step Gut Intelligence Align Practice, she no longer reacted to situations just to make them into something she needed them to be. Instead, she practiced the power of breathing, curiosity and detachment to align to her vision, values and goals. This created space for her to connect to her gut, heart and head so she could listen to the wisdom within.

Instead of looking outside herself for answers, as Rosemary often did when she consulted friends, she looked within because she realized no one had the answer for her but her. Only she knew the intricacies of her desires, values and boundaries. Only she could answer the question,

"How might I stay aligned to my vision, values and goals, considering this new information?"

By breathing more deeply, Rosemary could activate the vagus nerve to be more efficient in transporting the neurons and neurotransmitters from her gut to her heart and head-brain. As a result, she can now analyze and articulate the unconscious knowing from her gut while considering what she values and the variables given. Her head-brain would allow her to use language and reasoning to present possibilities to align her to her vision, values and goals—and she would become clear, calm and confident as a result of this inner knowing.

Rosemary was learning how Gut Intelligence, a form of mindfulness, contrasts with making impulsive decisions or getting stuck in analysis paralysis. Through continued practice of these steps, Rosemary was beginning to feel the difference between the times she was connected to herself and the times she was not.

Rosemary was beginning to understand the art of decision-making with increased Gut Intelligence—meaning that we allow our gut to alert us, our heart to remind us and our head-brain to clarify for us how we might align to our vision, values and goals in any given situation. By being aware of our unconscious gut cues and heart desires, we can ask our head-brain to answer our problem-solving question, "How might I stay aligned to my vision, values and goals, considering this new information?"

Increasing Your Gut Alert and Navigation Skills

When we pay attention to our gut alert, we find the guidance we need to navigate what isn't always clear to us at first. Increasing our gut alert and navigation skills allows us to notice the subtle, but important, cues at the tip of the iceberg that tell us:
"Yes...this is for me!"
"No...this is not for me!"
"Maybe...this could be for me with a few changes!"

For example, you may think you want that high paying job and promise of career advancement. But, as the offer comes in, you notice you have a pit in your stomach. You wonder, "Why?" Only you know the answer to this, and you will get that "a-ha" knowing when you slow down enough to wonder. When you slow down and wonder, you synthesize the gut alert with your heart's desire. Your mind can then put the pieces of the puzzle together and clarify the possibilities to get what you want, considering what you value.

Perhaps you did not consider your value of remaining flexible and available for your growing children. Does this mean you shouldn't take the corporate job? Maybe this could be the job for you if you negotiated flex time or working from home. Why go into a fight or flight reaction and say yes or no without a collaborative conversation first?

Or maybe you found a house you like, in the location you want, but it doesn't have as many bedrooms as you need. Maybe this could be the house for you with a few changes. Why quickly drop to the bottom-line and say yes or no if you love everything else about the house, can get it for the right price and close off that open spaced-den to make another bedroom?

Or perhaps you are thinking about leaving your job because you don't feel valued. You don't believe your talent is fully aligned to your job description or the goals. Before saying, "Yes, I'll stay," or "No, I'm going to look for another job," perhaps you can say to yourself, "Maybe I will sit down with my boss and discuss how I might align my talents to fit the company goals and negotiate a flex schedule to meet my personal needs."

Or, maybe you are in a relationship where one of you is more social than the other. Instead of concluding, "No, this is not a fit," what if you thought, "Maybe it could work if we could figure out a way to honor both our needs?"

These are some of the questions Rosemary had spinning in her mind as she tried to analyze decisions that were right for her talent, the time she wanted with her kids, and her relationship. When she increased her Gut Intelligence and paid more attention to her gut alert that told her adjustments were necessary for her happiness, she was more able to navigate these obstacles with a, "How might we..?" attitude. Proposing this problem-solving question to both her boss and her boyfriend could potentially help her stay in alignment with her vision, values and goals.

Instead of reacting and throwing the baby out with the bath water by dropping to the bottom-line and saying yes or no, Rosemary considered the desires of her heart and the possibilities to align to what she wanted most: talent alignment, time with the kids, and more time to relax and re-charge her batteries. For Rosemary, this meant a change in job description, more flex time at work, and more relaxation time with her boyfriend—as well as time alone. While she also wanted a thriving career and relationship, Rosemary now knew she didn't want either at the expense of her being a great mom and person who took time for herself. Realizing what she valued most allowed her to ask her boss, "How might we make some adjustments to my job description so I can better align my talents to the company goals?" and, "How might I have some more flex time so I can work more from home?"

Rosemary also formed questions for her boyfriend: "How might we be less scheduled and have more quiet time at home so I can recharge my batteries?" and "How might I get a night or two free so I can have some 'me' time?" Forming these problem-solving questions helped Rosemary raise her level of awareness and intention on what she wanted to create in her life. It also helped her let go of the attachment to lesser values so she could realize her greater potential and alignment.

For Rosemary, like all of us, this required letting go of any attachments to how it "should" be and what she "should" be capable of doing. This was a struggle for her, because she was conditioned to believe she could be there for everyone and sacrifice herself whenever needed. Rosemary had begun to see that when she lived with this unconscious bias and belief, she was not her best self. She would become burned out and resentful of others she perceived were demanding of her. What she learned was that it was not their fault—she was the one who had to set boundaries and ask for what she needed.

Without this realization, Rosemary often fell short of delivering everything she promised her boss, kids and boyfriend. When they were disappointed, she would say she didn't have enough time. What Rosemary was beginning to realize was that her gut would alert her before she made a commitment that she was over-committing, but she kept telling herself she would figure it out somehow.

Rosemary is now listening to her gut to alert her and her inner navigation system to consider other possibilities rather than simply saying yes or no. She is learning how to increase her Gut Intelligence by resisting the temptation to allow black-and-white thinking to rule her life. Increased Gut Intelligence means she can honor her gut alert, slow down enough to consider what she values most, and engage others in clarifying possibilities she otherwise could not see.

Gut Intelligence MEDITATION Practice

To help Rosemary get to the root cause of her tendency to people-please, we probed a bit into her past to find her unconscious bias and belief. She told me that when others demanded a lot from her and she began to believe she could not do it all, she would eat starchy foods and sweets.

I asked her when she began this habit, and she said it was at an early age. Probing further, I discovered she was the oldest of six kids and was often asked to take care of her siblings and the house while her parents went to work.

She said she would "treat herself" to potatoes, cupcakes, ice cream and chips as a way of rewarding herself for giving so much to the family. While she said, "Running the show had its perks," I sensed a sadness in her and that she believed she had no choice in the matter.

Today, when others are needy and want her help, Rosemary goes to this unconscious memory and belief that tells her she must sacrifice herself to help others in need. Breaking this reactive pattern requires learning a new response when others are demanding her help.

To assist Rosemary in increasing her Gut Intelligence so she could make a deeper connection with herself, I taught her the Gut Intelligence MEDITATION. The Gut Intelligence MEDITATION Practice is different from the Gut Intelligence ALIGN Practice. Where the ALIGN Practice is for more effective decision-making in the moment, the MEDITATION Practice is for deeper listening to oneself in order to experience a breakthrough or transformation when we feel stuck.

Here is how I instructed Rosemary:

Gut Intelligence MEDITATION Practice
Step 1: Practice your BREATHING
To prepare yourself for a deeper connection, breathe in the following way:
- Three breaths in the nose and out the mouth to the heart space, as slowly as you can
- Three breaths in the nose and out the mouth to the upper diaphragm, as slowly as you can
- Three breaths in the nose and out the mouth to the center of the gut, as slowly as you can

In this exercise, we are slowing down our brainwaves to alpha so we can make the vagus nerve more efficient and open up the corpus callosum in the brain. This helps us make a connection between the gut, heart and head.

Step 2: Practice your FOCUS
Focus on a problem-solving question like, *"How might I stop eating food when I am stressed about meeting others' expectations?"*

Step 3: Practice your LISTENING
Listen *AUDITORILY:* Bend to your left ear. *What do you hear your still-small voice saying to you?*
Listen *VISUALLY: What do you see in your mind's eye?*
Listen to your *GUT: What is your gut telling you is true?*

When we were done with the Gut Intelligence MEDITATION Practice, Rosemary told me she knew this strategy of over-eating not only kept her from speaking her truth, it also made her put on too many extra pounds—which she later loathed, perpetuating a judgmental cycle towards herself.

When I asked her how she was going to deal with the next request that walked through her door, she laughed and shouted out, "I got this! I'm going to take a deep breath and do the 3-Step Gut Intelligence ALIGN Practice to align to what I want most. To consider their needs, I will ask, 'How might we consider your needs and mine in this situation?' This will be a huge shift from me automatically saying 'yes' as I have done in the past!"

To end the session, I asked her what she now knew about her tendency to people-please. She responded, "When I was younger, I believed I didn't have a choice—I had to help whoever was in need. Now I do have a choice, and I can breathe deeply and connect with myself before I commit to anything or anyone."

How to Increase Your Locus of Control and Align to Your Vision, Values and Goals

In order to stay aligned to your vision, values and goals, you must increase your locus of control. A person with an internal locus of control believes that he or she can influence events and their outcomes, while someone with an external locus of control blames outside forces for everything. This concept was brought to light in the 1950s by Julian Rotter.

It is inevitable that we will face twists and turns in the road, obstacles, losses, difficult people and difficult situations as we navigate our way to our vision. If we take personal responsibility for our responses to these challenges and engage our Gut Intelligence, we will exhibit greater mastery over this difficult terrain.

If we are raised, however, by strict, overbearing and rigid parents who did not engage us in two-way conversations, we may have developed an external locus of control. An external locus of control makes us believe we are powerless, believing the power is outside of ourselves. This creates an internal voice of self-doubt instead of confidence when we try to make decisions in alignment with our own Gut Intelligence.

While this struggle may be more obvious when looking at Rosemary and her tendency to over-accommodate, Fred struggles with his locus of control too. We often don't see this the struggle with people like Fred, who mask their vulnerability by becoming more vocal and fighting for what they want—compared to Rosemary, who tends to lose her voice and accommodates. Where Fred yells and takes the reins of control, Rosemary lets go of her own voice and feels the need to please someone else. Both are reacting, because deep down inside they each feel powerless.

When unconscious fears like these penetrate our thinking and being, we can end up trying so hard to control the outcome in the immediate sense that we lose the bigger vision and alignment to our values. This was true for both Rosemary and Fred, as both had an unconscious need to regain the sense of power they lost in childhood. For Fred, he has an unconscious belief that he was not enough. This resulted from the rejection he felt from his father, who didn't know how to connect with him because he was different.

As a result, Fred was always striving to prove his significance to his board and the community. When results were unfavorable, he felt powerless to prove his worth. We increase our locus of control when we heal the unconscious belief inside that tells us we are not enough to affect the change we want.

To heal this wound and increase your locus of control, do the following:

7 Steps to Increase Your Locus of Control:
1) **Create a vision for your life.** Be sure you understand the "why." If you cannot define this, you may have this vision for unconscious reasons. Your "why" should be tied to something you love.
2) **Create your values.** Prioritize them. Create a storyline to explain what matters most to you.
3) **Define 3-5 Goals**. Be specific and be sure they are realistic and measurable.
4) **Create an action plan**. Outline who will do what by when.
5) **Focus on what you can control.** When appropriate, engage others and ask,
   "How might we create results?"
6) **Practice Gut Intelligence:** Make adjustments when your gut alerts you to change.
7) **Hold yourself accountable** with an accountability group and support system.

In reviewing the above steps, Fred admitted he glossed over many of them to create a self-fulfilling prophecy that he didn't have control. To gain more alignment to his vision, values and goals, he practiced having each of his department managers engage their employees and align them by creating an action plan to contribute to the goals. He would have them do this by having the managers ask, "How might we create results?" By engaging employees in this collaborative discussion, they would feel they were honored as viable talent required for the company's success. This would create ownership in the results up front.

Many business owners and leaders like Fred do not understand how they create this self-fulfilling prophecy that tells them, "If it's meant to be, it's up to me!" While they may appear controlling on the outside, it is really because they are feeling powerless on the inside.

Here are some tips to help you create your vision so you can have a greater locus of control, knowing your employees are all aligned in the same direction.

Tips for Creating Your Vision Statement:

1. Focus on what you love and the legacy you wish to leave
2. Face off self-doubt
3. Get curious
4. Write your vision in 14 words or less

Here are some popular vision statements to help you write yours:

"*A Hungry Free America*" (Feeding America)

"*To Leave a Sustainable World for Future Generations*" (The Nature Conservancy)

"*A World Where Everyone has a Decent Place to Live*" (Habitat for Humanity)

"*We envision a world where all people can create opportunity for themselves and others*" (Kiva)

Next, to create a greater locus of control, we want to create our values and align our employees to them. Values are what we deem is important and the standards to which we hold ourselves. While Fred had his values listed on a plaque on the wall, many of his employees did not understand how these values were used to make decisions. In fact, it often seemed that one value was compromised for another, so eventually no one took the values seriously.

I asked Fred to choose 5-10 values from the list below and

articulate how he wanted these values to be considered in decision-making. By sharing how they were to be upheld in decision-making, Fred would take more personal responsibility in ensuring the values were understood.

VALUES:

Following is a list of three different types of values: Physical, Organizational and Psychological.

Physical Values

___**Accuracy**
- Precision, exactness, and conforming to fact in details of work.

___**Cleanliness and Orderliness**
- Offices, facilities, equipment, raw material and finished product inventory, etc.

___**Maximizing Resources**
- Improving utilization of time, money, equipment, materials, space, people, etc.

___**Punctuality and Timeliness**
- To work and meetings, returning from breaks and lunch, replying to phone calls & emails, etc.

___**Quality of Products and Services**
- Presentation, functionality, speed, suitability, reliability, life span, courtesy, friendliness, etc.

___**Regularity**

- Meetings, reports, sales calls, performance reviews, etc.

___**Reliability**

- Systems or people who consistently produce the same results. Dependability.

___**Responsiveness**

- The speed and accuracy our employees respond to our internal and external customer.

___**Safety**

- Facilities, products and vehicles for employees, vendors and customers.

Organizational Values

___**Accountability**

- How we ensure individuals, departments and divisions perform and create results.

___**Alignment**

- Cooperation between departments in terms of activities, systems and goal achievement.

___**Collaboration (Teamwork)**

- Individuals, departments, divisions, and branches working in alignment to the goals.

___**Communications**

- Collaborative communication for the purpose of clarity, accuracy, timeliness and efficiency.

___**Discipline**

- Adherence to company policy, rules, systems, procedures, schedules, standards, ethics, etc.

___**Employee Engagement**

- To make suggestions, develop plans, and make decisions in alignment to the goals.

___**Integration**

- Smooth operation between different levels of the organization for goal alignment.

___**Standardization and Systemization**

- Making forms, procedures, reports, performance evaluations and communication consistent.

Psychological Values

___**Continuous Improvement**

- The ability for the company to develop and incorporate ways to improve itself.

___**Creativity and Innovation**

- Open-mindedness in developing new products, systems, methods, technology and strategies.

___**Customer Delight**

- The positive emotional response and joy that a customer feels from interacting with the company's people, products and services.

___Decisiveness

- In solving problems, planning, executing plans and committing to decisions once made.

___Integrity & Respect

- Keeping to one's word, promises and agreements in a truthful for the good of the all.

___Possibility-thinking and problem-solving

- The ability to see obstacles and bring possibility-thinking to solve issues and align to goals.

___Service to Society

- Focus and contribution to community welfare and developmental needs.

___Talent Alignment

- Tapping into employee talent to align it to the vision, values and goals for mutual growth.

While Fred was creating his vision and values for his business and engaging his employees in this alignment, Rosemary was working on values for her personal life. She was also engaging her kids, boss and boyfriend to understand and support her. Both were increasing their locus of control by articulating their vision and values up front.

Next, it was time for both of them to set goals so they could be more conscious of the decisions which would help them align to their vision and values.

For Rosemary, I had her outline goals for these 7 areas of her life:

7 Personal Goals:
1) Vocational
2) Financial
3) Relational
4) Physical
5) Emotional
6) Mental
7) Spiritual

Here's what Rosemary decided, based on her assessment and the insight she gleamed from our coaching session:

Rosemary's Personal Goals:
Vocational: Create a recognizable brand at work (How do I add value?)
Financial: Increase income by 20% and save 30%
Relational: Create more mutually supportive relationships
Physical: Relax and exercise more

Emotional: Don't over-commit

Mental: Practice possibility-thinking (and it doesn't always have to be me!)

Spiritual: Have more faith and less fear

For Fred, I had him focus on common work goals he needed to consider. I advised him to have three to five goals and to start with a one-year forecast. In the future, we would go out as far as three to five years.

<u>Work Goals:</u>
1. *Revenue*
2. *Profitability*
3. *Efficiency and Effectiveness*
4. *Customer Service and Satisfaction*
5. *Culture*
6. *New Products and Services*
7. *Market Share and Reach*
8. *Innovation*
9. *Employee Hiring and Retention*
10. *Growth*

After facilitating an online assessment to engage his employees in evaluating the company's needs, Fred decided on the following goals:

Fred's Company Goals:

Revenue: Increase by 20%

Customer Service and Satisfaction: Create raving fans by delivering on promises

Culture: Increase effective decision-making and goal alignment
Increase market reach by 20%

Once Rosemary and Fred had an overriding statement for each of their goals, it was time to create an action plan to support this achievement. An action plan outlines who will do what, and by when, to achieve one particular goal. This is the step most people miss. Instead of charting out their plan, they often resort to a daily to-do list. The problem with a to-do list is it often gets us out of synch with our goals. This is because we often do the activities that are not important but seem urgent.

Action Plan Template

Goal:

What	Who	By When
1.		
2.		
3.		
4.		
5.		
6.		
7.		
8.		
9.		
10.		

An action plan helped both Rosemary and Fred increase their locus on control for many reasons. First, they could be proactive in strategizing how to reach their goals rather than reactive when the goals were not met. This was an important benefit—especially for Fred, who tended to react when results were not optimal. The action plan was also a benefit for Rosemary, who often felt like she had to rescue people who didn't plan well and desperately asked for her help. By using this tool to think out personal responsibility, Rosemary could spare herself from over-responsibility.

Don't Depend on Your Happenings for Your Happiness

Creating a game plan, including articulating the vision, values and goals—was most helpful for Fred and Rosemary in gaining a greater locus of control. After this exercise, in order to be their best selves while achieving their goals, both would have to learn how to not depend on their happenings for their happiness.

I shared with Rosemary and Fred how scientists have determined that our level of happiness is a result of a complex interaction of the following:

1. Our predisposed genetic makeup
2. What we choose to think about
3. Our behaviors
4. How we spend our time
5. Our life circumstances

While scientists believe a portion of our happiness is due to our predisposed genetic make-up, much of our happiness is due to our thoughts and the behaviors we choose. According to the thought model below, our thoughts create feelings, and these feelings create behavior choices and results (our life circumstances).

I worked with Fred and Rosemary to show them how they could increase their happiness by becoming consciously aware of their thoughts. I gave them both the same example, seen below:

THOUGHT MODEL

Situation: An important employee quits

Thought:

 Old thought: Fred would have panicked in the past, telling everyone how to fill the gap.

Rosemary would have seen the gap and jumped in to help.

 New thought: Both now engage their teams and ask, "How might we fill this gap?"

Feeling: Empowered and confident (previously stress and a sense of being overly responsible)

Behavior: More collaborative (instead of controlling)

Results: More engagement and better results

The Thought Model showed Rosemary and Fred how to create more happiness, and results, in their lives by simply changing their thoughts in response to a situation. When they realized it was their thoughts that created their subconsciously anxious feelings, not the circumstances, they took ownership of how they chose to respond verses react. By responding with a "how might we…?" question, both Fred and Rosemary could increase their Gut Intelligence and address issues early on.

While both agreed the Thought Model was helpful, Fred admitted he missed the rush of adrenalin he often felt from being angry and judgmental. He admitted, "I loved the way it fueled me, and others, to move forward!" I shared with Fred how he was withdrawing from the chemical (cortisol) rush he was used to getting when he went into a fight or flight reaction. This chemical release can become very addicting and can make us believe it is an effective way to react. However, this fight and flight reaction gives us decreased blood flow to the brain—especially to the frontal cortex, where most of our possibility-thinking exists. While our reaction may create short-term effects on results, they are generally not lasting effects or have a positive impact on results.

While it is important to understand the wisdom of our emotions, it is equally important to understand our mindset that created the emotions to begin with. Circumstances don't create emotions—our thoughts do. When we get that gut alert, we are reminded to listen. Anxiety, which is fear produced in the body, tells us to proceed with caution. By understanding what produced this gut alert, we can become more enlightened on how to make an effective decision in alignment with our vision, values and goals.

Instead of increasing our ability to hear our gut alerts, many doctors are simply prescribing antidepressants and anxiety medication when their patients are feeling depressed or anxious. It is true that in some cases, patients need to get chemically balanced. But new research tells us much of this dis-ease is formed in the gut and can be repaired there through clean eating and listening to oneself.

A new government survey found that the number of Americans who say they've taken an antidepressant over the past month rose 65 percent between 1999 and 2014. The 2013 Medical Expenditure Panel Survey (MEPS) said one in six U.S. adults reported taking a psychiatric drug such as an antidepressant or a sedative. The report found women were twice as likely to use antidepressants than men: Showing 16.5 percent of females compared to just under nine percent of males. (E.J. Mundell, Health Day, August 16, 2017)

Practice Gut Intelligence to Increase Discernment and Decrease Dis-ease

We can change our thoughts and choose happiness every day when we increase our ability to listen to our inner voice. This inner voice is not our ego voice, it is our authentic self and higher consciousness—or as some say, "God's voice" or "the Holy Spirit." Whether you subscribe to a more psychological or spiritual perspective, aligning to what we love—our vision—is always better than aligning to our fear.

As we learn to increase our Gut Intelligence, we begin to increase our discernment between the voice of the ego (fear) and the voice of our higher consciousness (love). I call this level of higher consciousness "Intuitive Alignment." I believe intuition is the recognition of our spirit-self within. Five levels of Gut Intelligence allow us to connect with the spirit-self within to guide us to Intuitive Alignment:

Five Levels of Gut Intelligence:
- Level 1: Unawareness
- Level 2: Judgment and Self-doubt
- Level 3: Self-awareness
- Level 4: Detachment
- Level 5: Intuitive Alignment

While these levels of Gut Intelligence represent our wisdom to know the truth and our guts to do something about it, staying at Level 5, Intuitive Alignment, is difficult. When situations and people trigger our fear and attachment to outcomes, we often slip back into decreased Gut Intelligence.

In order to increase our Gut Intelligence and restore our Intuitive Alignment, we need to again let go of our attachments to preconceived conditions for happiness and love. The good news is that as you practice Gut Intelligence, you are aware when you have slipped back to these lower levels of being. The more you practice Gut Intelligence, the more you will recognize the cues that tell you to detach once again.

Below you will find a description of each of these levels of Gut Intelligence to help you identify where you are in every moment.

5 Levels of Gut Intelligence
Level 1: Unawareness is a state of consciousness where we feel the ping in our gut that alerts us, but we assume it was the situation or person triggering us. As a result, we often go into a fight or flight behavior to deal with people or situations. This state of awareness does not take a deeper dive into understanding why our gut was pinged, how to align to our heart's desires, or what to say or do

about a situation. This is the state of awareness of unconscious drama.

Level 2: Judgment and Self-doubt is a state of awareness where we are aware of our pain, but we believe others are causing it. As a result, there is a lot of projection onto others, believing they need to change for our unhappiness. We feel the gut alert and know what is occurring is not in alignment with our heart's desires, but we believe the answer, and power, are outside of ourselves. In this stage, we blame others and have self-doubt that we can do anything to make the situation better.

Level 3: Self-awareness means we become aware of what's not working in our lives, what triggers us, and how our ego steps in to react or take control. By noticing our own personal patterns of reaction, we can detach from our need to take things personally or control the outcome. It's important to make this observation without self-judgment.

Level 4: Detachment allows us to see more clearly how our need for safety, security, love and belonging are causing us pain. By observing our fears of how we may not be what we hoped for, we can detach from this fear and simply observe what is happening. This freedom of thought enables curiosity and better choices.

Level 5: Intuitive Alignment occurs when we ask a curious, "How might I (or we)...?" question. By asking, and then letting go of control, we align to the spirit-voice within rather than our ego voice. Because we no longer have the need to be right or in control, we can surrender to this spirit within for guidance. This results in better choices in alignment to our soul's vision, values and goals.

Understanding these levels of Gut Intelligence helped Fred and Rosemary to see what level of consciousness they were operating in and what was causing their unconscious reactions.

Both admitted that when they reacted, it was because they were operating at Level 2: Judgment and Self-doubt. While Fred tended to be more judgmental and Rosemary had more Self-doubt, both understood how their unconscious fears stifled their alignment to their greatest self. Fred's unconscious fear resulted in the mindset of, "If it's meant to be, it's up to me! They cannot create results as well as I can!" Rosemary's unconscious fear became a habitual thought pattern of, "If it's meant to be, it is up to me—because no one will pitch in or support me!" This resulted in both having a difficult time letting go, trusting and allowing others, and the Universe, to help them.

With their new understanding of how Gut Intelligence helps us to see possibilities beyond our automatic responses, both Fred and Rosemary became committed to detaching from their fears and becoming more intuitively aligned.

SECTION II

8 Spiritual Principles to Help You Align to Your Vision, Values and Goals

Overview: Becoming Your Best Self on Your Journey to Your Vision, Values and Goals

Once we arrive at Intuitive Alignment, we recognize the difference between operating from our ego and our spirit-self. Instead of seeing ourself as a human having a spiritual experience, we see ourself as a spirit having a human experience. This is a shift in mindset and way of being.

In the pages to follow, you will find principles that will help you achieve greater happiness as the result of your Intuitive Alignment. This means your happiness may not look like you thought it would, because it will not be predicated on your happenings. Instead, there will be a sense of being open, trusting and allowing for life to unfold while you hold the intention to manifest your vision, values and goals.

This may mean that some of your ambitions are never realized as you thought they would be. This does not mean you didn't ask hard enough, believe hard enough or receive well enough. It also doesn't mean you weren't good enough or somehow got it wrong. It just means you were supposed to have an experience to further your spirit's self-development. Maybe you are developing your ability to forgive, let go and learn a lesson. Or maybe someone you love doesn't love you back. Both could be opportunities to stay open-minded and curious about the next chapter in your life.

Following are the 8 Spiritual Principles you will learn in the following pages, and you will observe how Fred and Rosemary apply them in their lives:

Principle 1—*Be Humble*
Principle 2—*Ask, Believe and Receive*
Principle 3—*Forgive, Let Go and Learn*
Principle 4—*Stay Open-minded and Get Curious*
Principle 5—*Practice Gratitude*
Principle 6—*Embrace Grace and Synchronicity*
Principle 7—*Focus on Your Vision and Desire*
Principle 8—*Access Your Power*

By applying the Spiritual Principles, you will learn to be your best self as you achieve your vision, values and goals. This comes easier to you when you operate at Level 5, Intuitive Alignment, because you are abiding in your spirit-self, not your ego-self. According to Sigmund Freud, the ego is the part of our personality and the rational part of our mind that mediates the demands of self. This ego-self is our identity, made up of our own construction and based on our beliefs, personality, abilities and acquisitions. The ego hides behind descriptions of our identity and is very attached to outcomes to feed its purpose.

When we are operating at Level 5, Intuitive Alignment, we are abiding in the spirit-self, listening to the purity of the still-small voice inside. This is the voice that offers us the Fruits of the Spirit, explained in the Bible in Chapter 5 of the book of Galatians: "But the Fruit of the Spirit is love, joy, peace, patience, kindness, goodness, faithfulness, gentleness and self-control."

At Level 5, Intuitive Alignment, we meet the contrast between our spirit-self and our ego-self. This is where we become discerning between the still-small voice (which is based in love) and the chattering of our mind (which is rooted in fear).

SPIRIT	**EGO**
Love	Fear
Joy	Grief
Peace	Stress
Patience	Judgment
Kindness	Control
Goodness	Selfishness
Faithfulness	Disregard
Gentleness	Hard-heartedness
Self-control	Self-indulgence

When we look at our society, our corporate cultures, and even the dynamics in many families, we see the ego at work more often than the Fruits of the Spirit. Shifting towards the spirit requires us to operate from love verses fear. When we operate from love verses fear, we tap into the power of our spirit-self rather than our ego-self.

Practicing the Principles for Spiritual Alignment helps us to choose our spirit-self in our thoughts and interactions with others. When we make that choice, we gain the Fruits of the Spirit, which is where we will access our true power.

Some say the Fruits of the Spirit mean the Holy Spirit within us that wants to have control of our lives. Instead of working hard by the works of your flesh, what if you worked smart by the fruits of your spirit? Relying on our own logic and ego to lead your life impedes the leadership of this Holy Spirit in our lives.

As we begin with the mindset of what we love, verses fear, we approach our vision, values and goals differently. We have a choice to approach our destination by our spirit (love) or our ego (fear). Below you will see how the 8 Spiritual Principles will produce the Fruits of the Spirit and why developing these practices will benefit you.

How the 8 Spiritual Principles Produce the Fruits of the Spirit

PRACTICE	FRUIT OF THE SPIRIT
#1: Be Humble	*Love and joy*
#2: Ask, Believe and Receive	*Peace*
#3: Forgive, Let Go and Learn	*Patience*
#4: Stay Open-minded and Get Curious	*Kindness*
#5: Practice Gratitude	*Goodness*
#6: Embrace Grace and Synchronicity	*Faithfulness*
#7: Focus on Your Vision and Desire	*Gentleness*
#8: Access Your Power	*Self-control*

While we never permanently arrive at Level 5, Intuitive Alignment, you will know when you are de-railed into your ego mindset. While the ego often feels agitated, when we are aligned to our spirit-self we feel love, joy and peace. This transformation within you is not caused by your circumstances or the people around you. It is caused by you letting go of your attachments to outcomes and experiencing the Fruits of the Spirit, regardless of your circumstances.

When we surrender our ego-self to abide in our spirit-self, we begin to observe the unfoldment of life with pure observation and no judgment. From this state of being, we are living by the Fruits of the Spirit: love, joy, peace, patience, kindness, goodness, faithfulness, gentleness and self-control. No longer is our ego—whose personal identity is always threatened or tested because of its own attitude of entitlement—running the show. Instead, we are practicing our 8 Spiritual Principles so we can be our best selves as we achieve our vision, values and goals.

Principle 1—BE HUMBLE

The Gateway to Your Connection and Calling

Rosemary and Fred are not alone in thinking that love and happiness are conditions of circumstance. After all, look at the shows, media messages, Norman Rockwell photos, and songs that tell us this is true—like the song says, "You're not somebody until somebody loves you..."

Believing that everything is a condition of circumstance, Rosemary had been chasing the illusion of love and happiness as though it were outside of herself. This created a people-pleaser style of relating to get the love she so wanted. Because she believed love and happiness were outside of herself, and predicated on conditions, she missed out on deeper love and joy provided by the connection with her spirit-self. In order to get this connection, Rosemary needed to practice Spiritual Principle 1—*Be Humble.*

Fred was working on Spiritual Principle 1 too, but he was not as worried about his love life as he was about his work. Because his worth came from his work, he unconsciously feared that if he was not successful, he would be a nobody. Deep down inside, he feared that he was more of a Charlie Brown than Superman—and it was only a matter of time before people would figure that out!

Both Rosemary and Fred needed to practice being humble so they could experience the gateway to their connection with their spirit-self and get out of all the ego trappings in their minds. Fred was especially interested in finding his vision for his life so he could align more love and joy instead of always feeling so stressed out. While Rosemary felt she was in the right career, for her it was a matter of humbling herself to listen to the moment-by-moment guidance within so that she would no longer try to be everything to everyone else.

In order for both Fred and Rosemary to humble their ego-voices, they both decided to do a little deeper work to find their origins. Fred discovered that when he was seven years old, he declared that he wanted to be a veterinarian. He always loved animals, and all he ever wanted to do was go to the zoo, the pet store, and play with the neighborhood stray animals. His parents, however, owned a family business and didn't have much time to nurture Fred's natural tendency towards animals—they didn't even allow him to have a pet in the house. Beginning at a young age, Fred was told he would take over the business when his father retired.

Fred admitted to feeling this calling as a veterinarian throughout his younger years but that he never wanted to tell anyone. He had seen the movie *One Flew Over the Cuckoo's Nest* and didn't want anyone thinking he was nuts! Everyone around him told him he had a blessed life—but for Fred, it was a trap that never allowed him to pursue his true passion and calling.

Because Fred was conditioned to believe he needed to take over the legacy and continue to support the family, he formed a mindset that said, "If it is meant to be, it is up to me!" Pride developed instead of humility, which made him begin to pull up his own bootstraps. The more Fred abandoned his own calling and connection with his inner self, the more his need to be recognized by others grew. This was no different from Rosemary, who abandoned herself in her daily decisions for the purpose of having others think she was so giving.

Both Fred and Rosemary were learning to slow down and make more of a connection within by humbling themselves and asking for guidance from their spirit-self. While Fred was not ready to consider quitting the family business yet, both were working on internal listening by breathing more deeply and asking themselves, "How might I handle this?" Both needed to practice asking for guidance in the day-to-day decisions before they could take the big leap and ask for a greater calling. Both admitted they often allowed for the day-to-day busyness to override this desire for connection. They said when they slowed down to listen within, they often felt guilty that they were not being more "productive."

I shared with them a passage from the Old Testament that addresses this struggle between our flesh and our spirit. In Ephesians 6:12, we hear, "For our struggle is not against enemies of blood and flesh, but against the rulers, against the authorities, against the cosmic powers of this present darkness, against the spiritual forces of evil in the heavenly places."

Lucifer (Satan), an angel and God's wisest creature ever created, is principally behind this ego-mindset. In Ezekiel 28:14, he is called "the anointed cherub." In Isaiah 14:12, we learn of Lucifer's choice—"I will take over heaven. I will be God!" The choice that Lucifer made is what we all face in original sin. Will we be in control and try to take over the will of Heaven and be God in our lives? That is pride, and pride is the fall. Or will we be humble and seek the connection and calling of our spirit?

There is free will, and the choice is ours.

Spiritual Principle 1 reminds us of our spiritual battle to be in control. Rosemary experienced this struggle when she was babysitting her five-year old granddaughter and called her up to take a bath. Her granddaughter resisted, until finally she jumped in the tub and was so happy that she didn't want to get out. After the bath, Rosemary's granddaughter admitted she liked feeling so clean and refreshed. This is how we feel when we spend time with our spirit-self. When we bathe in the spirit, we feel refreshed and clean!

We long to be separate, independent and in control—yet we want to be connected and loved.
We are afraid of humbling ourselves
for fear of what we may hear.

Rosemary and Fred were both learning that while humbling oneself can be difficult at first, through practice they can receive the Fruits of the Spirit: more love and joy in their lives. This was because they were not doing what they thought they "should" be doing. Being humble, they instead admitted they did not have all the answers and needed to go within to find out what it was they needed to know. This practice of humility brought them much love and joy.

Principle 2—ASK, BELIEVE AND RECEIVE

Creating an Honest Relationship with Self and Others

As Rosemary and Fred admitted, learning to listen to our inner voice can be rather scary at first. When we ask our spirit-self for direction, we step into the unknown—not knowing what we will hear. This is especially hard for people who pride themselves on their accomplishments and have formed a strong autonomous identity.

I assured Rosemary and Fred they weren't alone in this fear. Fear of the unknown is our number one stressor, according to the Holmes & Rahe Stress Scale. This fear makes us more stressed than if we knew for sure that something bad was going to happen. This is why we would rather focus on negative outcomes or try to do it on our own will than surrender and sit in the unknown, waiting for the spirit to work it out!

When looking at the top ten stressors, according to the Holmes & Rahe Stress Scale, they all have one thing in common: The stress of navigating the unknown.

Top Ten Stressors: (The American Institute of Stress)

Death of a spouse or child

Divorce

Marital separation

Imprisonment

Death of a close family member

Personal injury or illness

Marriage

Dismissal from work

Marriage reconciliation

Retirement

The unknown is a stressor for us because we often do not know how to navigate it. This can put us into a fight and flight response quickly—unless we practice Spiritual Principal 2—*Ask, Believe and Receive.*

As we practice Principle 2, it becomes more natural and we begin to realize we are not alone in dealing with the unknown. Rosemary admitted that practicing Principle 2 was beginning to help her tendency to people-please, as she would "ask" her spirit-self how to respond to others' requests before jumping in with her typical "yes!" This gave her the Fruit of the Spirit: peace.
Rosemary now consciously acknowledges this partnership by asking

her spirit-self:

"How might we navigate this unknown?"

Unfortunately, before we can hear the still-small voice, we must get past the chattering in our minds. This chattering is our fear—full of preconceived notions and thoughts of the worst possibilities of what could happen if we ask for guidance. Fred is struggling with Principle 2 because he is afraid that if he asks, he may hear, "You shouldn't be running the business!"—and he feels he is too old to start over in the career he missed out on as a veterinarian.

These are the moments when we must make a conscious choice: Will we believe our ego again and try to be in control, or will we practice Spiritual Principle 2 and Ask, Believe and Receive?

As Fred admits, it is not easy to give up the mind chattering and the ego aspect of oneself, which governs our perceived needs for safety, security, love and belonging. For him, these perceived needs were based on his parents' preconceived notions and desires for his life.

While they likely meant well, Fred now feels stuck, ripped off from his dream, and abandoned. The truth is, we are never abandoned.

While at times we believe we did not get what we wanted, life always gives us something else our heart and soul needed in order to grow.

Knowing that life always works out, we can believe, "This or something better is on its way!" With that mantra, we are open-minded to receive possibilities in ways we could not otherwise imagine.

Fred wanted to know if Principle 2 was like having a "Jeanie-in-a-bottle." I told him that it was more like having an effective parent. There were times my children wanted things they never got from me. For example, when they were 16 years old, they wanted a brand new car. They got a car, but it was used and didn't have all the bells and whistles they wished it had. They asked for something newer and believed they would get it, because most of their other friends received new cars at age 16. I told them they received a used car because I wanted them to *earn* their first brand new car—so they could experience the joy that brought! While they didn't buy into my reasoning at the time, they both now feel self-esteem from earning their own new cars.

I told Fred the point of my story was this: When we practice Principle 2—*Ask, Believe and Receive*, we must practice staying detached to the outcomes we imagined in our minds. If you are someone who sees specifically what something will look like, you may often be disappointed and miss the blessing in the outcome. This closed mindset can rob us of our happiness and prevent us from truly being happy. In order to master this principle, we must believe we are always receiving what is highest and best for us.

Both Rosemary and Fred are learning how to humbly ask, believe and receive. They are beginning to understand that this is different from asking with an entitled mentality. When we combine Spiritual Principle 1—*Be Humble* with Spiritual Principle 2—*Ask, Believe and Receive*, our way of asking shifts.

Being humble means we learn to welcome whatever we receive as we believe "thine will is my will for my higher good." When we believe our spirit-self has our higher good in mind, we can be at peace as we wait upon "this or something better."

As I explained this, Fred nodded his head, beginning to understand that perhaps he asked for the life he had in some way he hadn't yet understood.

Principle 3—FORGIVE, LET GO AND LEARN

Unconscious Beliefs and Biases Inhibit Our Ability to Surrender

We often think we need to forgive others when it is actually ourselves we need to forgive. We need to forgive ourselves for believing the present moment is offering us anything other than what we need to be happy and reach our potential. This means letting go of any preconceived notions of what love and happiness look like in our minds. When we forgive ourselves for believing we know what's best for us, we can let go and learn what we need to learn in order to live a life connected to our deepest spirit-self.

Now that Fred was in touch with his childhood dream and how his parents expected him to run the family business, he needed to practice Spiritual Principle 3—forgiving, letting go and learning what it was he needed to learn. Fred was feeling like a victim, at some level, until I challenged him to look at the perfect unfoldment of it all. I asked him, "What if it was meant to be that you were born into this family to experience what it was like to be a business owner. What if this was a perfect unfoldment to something you were supposed to do? What if you were given the Fruit of the Spirit—patience—along your journey? What would you see next?"

Transforming our victim-mindset requires patience, one of the Fruits of the Spirit. As we abide in our spirit-self, we receive this gift. Spirit reveals to us the perfection in what "is." Unfortunately, however, we battle with our ego once again, as it strives to gain control at each level of awareness in our unfoldment.

Spiritual Principle 3—*Forgive, Let Go and Learn* allows us to further see how our ego judges situations as "good" or "bad" instead of, "It is what it is. Now what do I need to let go of and learn?"

To help us practice Spiritual Principle 3: *Forgive, Let Go and Learn*, I told Fred and Rosemary how the ego was developed within them. This aspect of self was developed primarily between our ages of birth to eight years old, when we gave our authority away to someone else. We did this because we thought they had the key to making us feel safe, secure and loved. This could have been our parents, a community, a church or some other authority in our lives. Consequently, we took on their beliefs and biases so we could be a part of the group-think. This, of course, was all unspoken—so it was subtle. Now it is buried in our subconscious minds, causing limited thinking about how life "should" be.

Part of the evolution to connect with our spirit-self is to forgive ourselves for making someone else's beliefs and wishes more important than our own. We did this, of course, because we believed we had to in order to be safe, secure and loved by a group or community. Other times, we were the leader of that group-think and were intolerant when someone did not bend towards what we believed "should" be. Of course, most of us are not conscious of doing this to others. We only know we have needs and when they are not being met. This is how power and control struggles are formed in relationships.

Both Fred and Rosemary could remember times they spoke up and went against the norm. For Fred, it was a stern hold on expectations; with Rosemary, she faced her father's abuse when she didn't meet his expectations. While Fred's father wasn't an alcoholic like Rosemary's was, his stern position never let anyone else's contrary position be fully heard.

Both realized their relationships with their parents were based upon a strong power and control dynamic. Fred saw this in himself, admitting he frequently got that way with his employees when he was not pleased with results. Rosemary said she did the dance too, by withholding and getting an attitude when she thought she gave more than she was receiving. While Fred's style of relating was more dominant and competing, Rosemary's was more accommodating and passive-aggressive.

Due to their unconscious needs to control, they both needed to forgive themselves, let go of the past, and learn how to co-create differently in relationships. This would mean honoring their own spirit-self—as they honored the spirit in someone else.

Here are the common unconscious gender biases and beliefs that keep us stuck in power and control struggles instead of being our authentic selves:

MEN'S UNCONSCIOUS BIASES & BELIEFS

- If you are not strong, and if you are sensitive, you are a wimp (or gay)
- Your role is to be a provider and protector
- Your worth is your wealth

These beliefs leave men to believe they need to hide their authentic feelings and just "buck it up." It can also give them a false ambition to climb the ladder in order to provide and feel a sense of worth. Unfortunately, these societal beliefs inadvertently force them to look outside of themselves for safety, security, love and belonging. Stepping outside this norm is very difficult and takes much courage. The core bias and belief for men is this: Love means they must provide and protect their families!

WOMEN'S UNCONSCIOUS BIASES & BELIEFS

- If you are strong, you are a bitch
- You are the nurturer and emotional supporter of the family
- Your worth is your relationships

These leave women to believe they need to be more agreeable, not have an opinion or argue. While women believe they can go to work, they are always worried about being in balance, because they are told they are the primary nurturer and emotional supporter of the family. The core bias and belief for women is this: Love means they must take care of everyone around them!

Rosemary and Fred could now see how unconscious gender biases and beliefs kept them from going deeper within to surrender the needs of their ego. For Fred, this was the need to be a "provider." For Rosemary, this was her need to be "all-giving."

Both are now realizing they need to forgive themselves for being anything other than who they are. By letting go of these gender biases and beliefs, they can now realize who they are meant to be.

Principle 4—STAY OPEN-MINDED AND GET CURIOUS

Curiosity Bridges the Gap of Differences

If we were raised in a way that we were put into a box of preconceived expectations, we likely became closed-minded and judgmental. This is because we were not taught how to stay open-minded and curious when faced with differences.

Making the shift to more open-mindedness bridges the gap in our different perspectives. Unfortunately, however, if we were like Fred and Rosemary, we learned at a young age that communication was top down. This kept us from practicing Principle 4—*Stay Open-minded and Get Curious*. Instead of having this style of being and communicating modeled to us, we learned how to relate from our ego-self—that aspect of self that is closed-minded and wants to be in control.

When we abide in the spirit-self, we gain a Fruit of the Spirit—kindness. Kindness allows us to be more open-minded and curious with ourselves and with others. This develops a two-way communication where all are heard and considered. Someone who practices Principle 4 will ask:

"How might we work this out for the good of all?"

This question helps us let go of our grip on control, opens our minds, and gets us curious and kind toward others' needs.

Our ego-self, on the other hand, only thinks of "I"—"What do I want in this situation, and how will I get it?" There is no kindness to another person when we come from this perspective. Just as it isn't kind to others to leave their needs out of the equation, it isn't kind to leave ourselves out.

Rosemary gave this principle a lot of thought and admitted she was closed-minded and full of judgment when it came to others. She admitted that she believed others were not as giving and kind as she was, so she always had to fill the gap. With this realization, she laughed and said, "It's not kind to over-give because you think you are better than everyone else. That's my ego really only thinking about myself! Until now, I saw it the other way around—but the truth is, my people-pleasing is for my own self-importance!"

Because Rosemary was willing to be curious, she took her ego-self off the throne, opened her mind, and got curious about her role in the dynamic. She was able to admit that in the face of differences, she experienced fear and over-gave in order to control being seen, heard, considered and honored for her uniqueness. To begin applying Principle 4 immediately, Rosemary started to open her mind and get curious about how others could add value in any given situation so that they could feel important too. This allowed her to see possibilities she couldn't otherwise see.

Fred was less self-reflective and more curious about how to apply this principle in a practical way at work. He admitted that he became closed-minded and judgmental when the expenses exceeded the revenue—but that he felt justified in that reaction.

I shared with Fred three practical ways he could respond in order to become more open-minded and curious when he saw an unfavorable financial report:

1. Ask questions.
2. Listen for the root need.
3. Collaborate by asking, "How might we get our revenue to exceed our expenses?"

Fred and I discussed how being open-minded and curious would not only help him understand the root cause, but it would help him engage others in solving the problem. When we engage others, we honor their input and show kindness to their points of view.

But even though Fred knew exactly what I meant, he asked an honest question: "But what if you really believe you have the right answer and they do not? Then what? What good is it to practice an open and curious mind if it's not really open and curious?"

The fact that Fred could admit this inner struggle with his ego was a good thing. It was the beginning of enlightenment—he was being open-minded and curious about how he showed up with others! I praised him for not judging himself or just baring witness to what was happening within and around him.

I told him, "When we witness what 'is' without judgment, we give space for transformation.
I practiced principle 4 on the spot with Fred and became curious about the benefit he got from being closed-minded and judgmental. He told me he was rather bored with his job as president and CEO and enjoyed feeling needed.

Instead of trying to prove I was right about Spiritual Practice 4—*Stay Open-minded and Get Curious*, I chose to bridge the gap in our different perspectives by just practicing the principle myself in the moment. Instead of being judgmental about how Fred ran his business, I just remained curious. Curious about how he learned to be this way, curious about what he gained from it, curious about how others reacted, and curious about whether he would begin to open his mind to others more often.

While I didn't know what the outcome would be, it just felt good to practice staying open-minded and curious. It kept me from the ugly fearful and closed-minded way of being.

Principle 5—PRACTICE GRATITUDE

Detaching from Outcomes and Preconceived Notions

As we detach from the outcomes and preconceived notions of how things ought to be, we become more liberated and empowered. I was having to practice this principle myself, as my ego wanted so badly for Fred to become open-minded and more curious with his employees.

While my intentions may have been good, anytime we hold onto someone or something having to be a certain way, we do not allow for transformation to occur. This is because our ego-self, full of pride, does not make way for the spirit to do its thing!

Principle 5—*Practice Gratitude*, helps us to focus on appreciation for what is. As I practiced gratitude, I could see the goodness in Fred and his intention to be the best leader he could be. After all, Fred signed up for the ALIGN program himself. No one made him do it—he wanted to be his best self! It was the spirit's job, not mine (which was a tough one for my ego) to transform him in whatever way and timing was right for him. As I let go of trying to control the outcome and abided more in my own spirit-self, I was giving the Fruit of the Spirit: goodness. Goodness allowed me to let go of worrying about what had not already occurred and delight, with gratitude, in the progress already made. As I was allowing my spirit-self to guide me, I had this realization: This is exactly the struggle Fred had!

Realizing how I shared this shadow-aspect with Fred, my appreciation for his struggle grew. According to Carl Jung, the shadow is an unknown perceived inferiority that we project onto another. When we can simply observe what "is" in the other person, we begin to appreciate that aspect in ourselves and stop projecting it. This allows us to observe what is occurring with pure curiosity. It loosens our grip on a certain outcome, and we give up pride and control. Detaching from outcomes, and being grateful for what "is," allows our spirit to have control.

It's hard to just observe what "is" with gratitude when you aren't quite getting the results you want. I could see, however, a new perspective now: Tightly holding a grip on a certain outcome shows a level of pride and control. Detaching from outcomes, and being grateful for what "is," allows spirit to have control.

Practicing gratitude and detaching from the outcome, as we deem it ought to be, helps us live a happier life—because we can get off others' backs and on with our own life. Rosemary chimed in on this aspect of the lesson and shared a time she struggled with being grateful. She explained how she worked hard to plan a baby shower at her friend's house, and it rained the whole day of the party. They could not do any of the outdoor activities she worked so hard to plan, and there could be no outside barbequing. She said, "Nothing turned out as expected, and I had a hard time being grateful."

I had empathy for Rosemary and gave out a big sigh when she told her story. I am a planner, too, and I could feel the disappointment she must have felt. It's okay to experience moments of disappointment like this, but we want to be sure we are not so attached that we aren't present in the moment. When we let go of our attachment to outcomes we thought we needed, we can then be open-minded enough to receive the unexpected gift. This allows us to be grateful for something other than what was originally planned or hoped for.

I asked Rosemary if there was any goodness that came out of this situation. She admitted she had wasted so much mind-energy on her disappointment and frustration that she hadn't really thought about what unfolded. This shift in mindset was helping her look beyond her preconceived notions in order to be grateful for the perfect unfoldment of life. By looking at what life had presented her, she could begin to appreciate all that occurred.

Principal 5—*Practice Gratitude* gave Rosemary the ability to see something she had previously missed. She recalled all the fun the group had sitting around and chatting with each other inside the house. She told me that a man and a woman who ended up sitting next to each other on the couch are now a couple. She also admitted she enjoyed having the time to really get to know a few guests she otherwise may not have had the time to talk with.

While we can all be disappointed when things don't go as planned, I reminded Rosemary of my favorite sayings:

"This or something better is on its way!"

This mind-mantra helps me be free from attachments to outcomes and preconceived notions—and be grateful for all that "is."

Gratitude is the quality of being thankful for all the good we receive instead of looking at what we didn't get. When we practice being grateful for the little things in life, we form a habit and can be more prepared to have the mindset of gratitude when we face bigger disappointments. When we are thankful, we not only show more goodness by focusing on what is good—we reap physical benefits as well.

Did you know that people who express more gratitude experience less aches and pains? Gratitude reduces toxic emotions, according to Robert A. Emmons, PhD., a leading gratitude researcher who has studied the link between gratitude and well-being. What he found was that gratitude increases happiness and decreases depression. As a result of gratitude, people are less aggressive and show more goodness to themselves and others, building self-esteem.

(Melanie Greenberg, PHD, "How Gratitude Leads to a Happier Life", Psychology Today, November 22, 2015)

It takes mental strength for us to focus on gratitude when things are seemingly not perfect—such as results being down for a month. In closing the session on gratitude, I asked Fred, "How could gratitude help you increase your revenue, even on the months when sales are down and expenses are up?"

After thinking about it for a moment, Fred answered, "We tend to wait until monumental moments to show gratitude. But when we focus on what is working and expand from that, we acknowledge the divine in others and what they are working hard to create. When I would come in and criticize what wasn't working, I stole their thunder and deflated their ego so that mine could feel good. Gratitude cultivates what is working, and what we focus on expands."

Fred had been listening, pondering and understanding the principles more than I realized.

Principle 6—EMBRACE GRACE AND SYNCHRONICITY

Stepping into the Unknown

Because we are a society that is used to having information at our fingertips, we can easily become entitled and expect to get answers from our inner voice immediately. Sometimes we do get an immediate answer, and sometimes we do not.

To tap into grace and synchronicity, we need to step into the unknown and have faith that the answer is coming. As we wait for grace and synchronicity to appear, our spirit-self is cultivating faithfulness. This is not wasted time in the waiting room, as stepping into the unknown and increasing our faithfulness makes the ego-self wane.

When we learn to step into the unknown and be content without answers, we receive grace and synchronicity. This does not mean we don't have any responsibility in achieving results—we do! Our job is to ask and receive guidance and gifts with an open and grateful mindset.

I said, "Easier said than done, right?" Both Fred and Rosemary nodded in agreement. Here are some of the tips I gave them to help them with Spiritual Principle 6:

1) **Create a Grace and Synchronicity Journal:**

    When you face an obstacle or desire a particular outcome, write about it. Journaling allows us to write about our anxiety, judgment, hopelessness and the temptation we feel—and our need to control the timing and outcome. As we write about our inner experience, we can better embrace grace and synchronicity. This allows us to have more faith and not settle for any answer. When we settle, it's often because we did not want to wait in the unknown. At some level, we know when anxiety or depression causes us to choose something just to avoid being in the unknown.

Fred could especially relate to this when it came to hiring employees. He often said when a need arose, they felt like they had to fill the spot right away. Whenever they made a rushed hiring decision and didn't listen to their Gut Intelligence or have faith that someone better would come along, they ended up with issues. Fred made a note to practice Spiritual Principle 6 regarding hiring.

Rosemary could see how Principle 6 might help her, too. She admitted that she did most things on her own and didn't let anyone help her—much less let in grace and synchronicity. She wondered,

"What would happen if I slowed down enough to look for it—what would I see?"

2) **Change Your Mindset:**

    What if you viewed the unknown as an adventure—something to explore and embrace? Would you enjoy the unknown more that way? People who are resilient and open-minded see the unknown through a different lens than those who tend to dread the unknown. Imagine if you said to yourself, "God must be preparing something big and wonderful for me! I cannot wait to see what grace and synchronicity have in store!"

Fred piped in, "Consciously engaging uncertainty will allow me to thrive in the unknown, where in the past I got agitated. The unknown challenges my ego, especially when it comes to revenue. If it's down, so am I. Instead of going to such a negative place, I am going to wonder how grace and synchronicity can help us bridge the gap in what we need!"

Fred clearly understood that as we embrace the unknown, we move away from our ego-self and become more aligned to our spirit-self. This occurs because we have to be curious about how to navigate uncharted waters.

Rosemary chimed in with a quote she knew from Albert Einstein: "Coincidence is God's way of remaining anonymous." She continued, "Where often believe we are experiencing random events, we are actually experiencing synchronicities. This just happened to me the other day, when I was feeling overwhelmed and decided I needed a contractor to help with a repair in the house. I was driving my car at the time, and I looked to the side of me on the highway—and there was a van advertising the type of contractor I needed. The phone number was simple to read and easy to memorize. I called them, and they were available immediately. As it turned out, he was one of my friend's brothers!"

Both Fred and I shared our own stories of grace and synchronicity. Some of our stories included:

- Thinking about a friend and hearing your inner voice telling you to call them—and right then, they call you.
- Hearing your inner voice tell you to look on the internet for a home, and the home you imagined in your mind's eye pops up and is available when you need it.
- You weren't going to go out of town, but when you did, you met a big client.
- You saw a post on Facebook and felt so impacted that you changed some of the things you were pondering about in your life.

These were just a few of the examples we shared on how grace and synchronicity worked in our lives. Carl Jung coined the term "synchronicity," defining it as a meaningful coincidence that has a low probability of being a random or chance event.

Waiting on God to fulfill his purpose is a form of grace. Romans 8:25b says, "That is why waiting does not diminish us, any more than waiting diminishes a pregnant mother. We are enlarged in the waiting. We, of course, don't see what is enlarging us. But the longer we wait, the larger we become, and the more joyful our expectancy."

When we practice Spiritual Principle 6—*Embrace Grace and Synchronicity*, we are more apt to look for it in our personal and work lives. By letting go of control, stepping in the unknown and having faith, we expand the space for grace and synchronicity to appear.

Principle 7—FOCUS ON YOUR VISION AND DESIRE
Feel How Great It Will Be When You Arrive!

Fred and Rosemary were now being changed from the inside out. Both were showing up differently in their stressful situations with more intention of the people they wanted to be. Next, it was time to bring their vision and desires for the future back into focus so they could integrate the ability to be present while aligning to what they wanted to create.

Focusing on vision and desire was going to look different now. Instead of fretting, "Can I make these results happen?!" they would approach their vision and desires with more of the Fruit of the Spirit: gentleness. Gentleness does not mean lack of focus or weakness. It means to approach our vision and desires with more lightness and less harshness.

Most people fret in the waiting room of life. When we are waiting for results to occur, we often worry. "Why?" I asked Rosemary and Fred. Rosemary jumped in to answer, "It's a habit! Worry fills a space in my mind so that I don't have to be in the unknown. I play the 'what if' game to try and control the outcome by thinking through every possible situation!"

To help Rosemary fill her mind with something more productive, I suggested she focus on the desire in her heart and the vision in her mind. I asked Fred, "How would you be different if you believed you would get the exact number you needed on the bottom of your monthly P&L next month?"

Fred admitted he spent a lot of time with worry in his mind, not the vision he desired. When his fears came true, he could say to himself, "See, I knew it!" While he didn't like the outcome, he admitted he liked being right.

Fred understood how he had a choice about his mindset. Would he fret about results, or focus on his vision and desire? We explored some of the options he had to focus on his vision and desire in order to see the shift in practical terms. To help him think of possible ways to do this, I asked him:

"How might you focus on your vision and desire to help increase revenue?"

Fred shared many ideas, which included:
1) "Spend more time with animals outside. This inspires and relaxes me, like it did when I was a kid. I am sure I would come up with ideas to share with my team."

2) "Don't work long hours just because I'm afraid I won't get the outcome I desire if I don't."
3) "When I feel anxious and uneasy, ask myself if I've picked up any cues at the tip of the iceberg I need to address now."
4) "If I'm thinking about work after hours, ask myself if there is a "how might we…?" question I need to meditate on."
5) "Meet with my managers weekly, and find out how they are engaging their employees in the goal of increasing revenue and decreasing expenses."

Fred and Rosemary were both realizing this fact: When we spend time worrying, we are not spending time focusing on how we might reach our vision. Instead of worrying about how things aren't unfolding, they would now focus on their vision and wonder how they would reach them.

When we wonder, instead of worry, we tap into the spirit-self who knows the answer.

Progress on our vision and goals makes us happier. We all know deep down inside what it is we want in order to be happy—but we need to train our minds to focus on our vision and desires instead of focusing on what we fear.

We can shift our focus and improve our results in these three ways:

1. Focus on your vision instead of where you currently are right now.
2. Focus on your desire instead of your fear.
3. Focus on strategy and goals instead of what is not working.

Fred knew he wanted more revenue than expenses, but his thoughts kept him from improving his situation. By getting clear on his vision, including how much revenue he expected and at what expense, he could help his team strategize to meet his goals.

Rosemary and Fred were both working on articulating their vision and desires. For Rosemary, it was less about money and more about emotional support. She had a boyfriend who wanted to take her out and wine and dine her all the time. What she wanted more than this was to have someone who was curious and caring about her workload and her need for support. Being a single parent and full-time executive was hard for Rosemary, so she envisioned her workload getting lighter so that she could enjoy being more present for herself and everyone around her.

By evaluating where they both were, and envisioning where they desired to be, both Rosemary and Fred could actively explore options to enlist the help of others in attaining their vision. At that point, they could establish a plan to give them more of the life they each wanted.

Principle 8—ACCESS YOUR POWER

Slowing It Down to Align

We often move through life like a jaguar racing through the McDonald's drive-through. What if instead you were looking at your life as a leisurely drive through the country, with a lovely picnic to be savored instead? Slowing down requires self-control, a Fruit of the Spirit, given to us when we spend more time with our spirit-self and focus on Principle 8—*Access Your Power*.

While I love technology, instead of helping us to be efficient, we often allow it to speed us up and cause distraction. When we are put on hold during a phone call, we often multi-task— searching our emails or opening Facebook. What if instead, we took a moment to just be with ourselves?

Being busy has become a badge of honor in our society. When people ask you, "How are you?" Instead of saying, "Fine, thank you!" most of us say, "Busy...oh I'm so busy!"

What if we answered the question by saying, "Actually, I have more time than I know what to do with because I figured out what my vision and desires are and now have the self-control to make decisions in alignment with them!" Of course, that would be a little odd to say—but my point is that if this is truly how we lived, we wouldn't be saying, "Oh, I'm so busy!" Wouldn't that be great if personal alignment became the norm for people? Everyone would have the ability to access their power in a healthy way by simply slowing it down so they could align to what they really wanted most!

Answering the question, "How are you?" with, "I'm so busy" is a mirror of our society's value of "doing" over just "being." While meditation has become popular in our culture, taking only 20 to 30 minutes a day to slow down and be with our spirit-self is still a challenge for many people.

- While mindfulness is growing in popularity, in 2017 only 14 percent of U.S. adults said they'd practiced yoga or meditation.
(Amy Norton, Healthday Reporter, November 8, 2018)

The western culture is built on the freedom to find our dreams. I believe in that value. Unfortunately, however, we have become a society that values materialism and individualism as a symbol of arrival. This makes it difficult to embrace the principle of slowing down and listening to ourselves.

I asked Fred and Rosemary to imagine this situation: They walk by two executive officers. One is engaged on the phone and actively working out a transaction. Another is sitting back in his chair, gazing out the window, thinking about how to effectively handle an employee who is not performing. Who would you be happier with at first glance?

Both Rosemary and Fred admitted it would be the first executive. When I asked why, they both admitted that at first glance, it would appear as though that executive was being more productive. We often think that slowing down means we are being unproductive. Our minds tell us to be disciplined and to do things step-by-step to get us where we want to go. I'm not saying discipline isn't also effective—it has its place in the execution stage. But what happened to the process of ready-aim-fire? Our society has adopted the process of fire-fire-fire—and we are creating an unnecessary fire drill in many cases.

Principle 8—*Access Your Power* means we can get to where we want to go more effectively with the Fruit of the Spirit: self-control. Self-control means we control the anxious emotions that tell us we always need to be busy to be worthy. Self-control means we no longer live by perspired action, only inspired action. This self-control comes from abiding more in our spirit-self. When we abide more in our spirit-self, we get clarity. Clarity is power.

This means instead of trying so hard to figure it out, we only ask our spirit-self one clear problem-solving question at a time and let the answer come to us.

Fred realized he is like many of us in society and feeds on instant gratification. This causes him to speed things up and work hard to get immediate results. In order to practice Principle 8—*Access Your Power*, Fred made a commitment to take up horseback riding and spend more time in the country. He knows slowing it down will help him get clear about what it is he wants and how to go about getting it.

Accessing our power occurs when we first connect with our navigation system—our Gut Intelligence, which leads us away from our ego-self and connects us to our spirit-self. We do this by first slowing it down and stepping into the present moment. At that point, we can hear that still-small gut alert, or whisper in our ear, that tells us to pay attention to the cues at the tip of the iceberg that need our attention.

When we slow down and breathe more deeply, we shift our brainwaves to alpha and move out of busy beta brainwaves. Neurotransmitters and neurons from our gut are now able to travel up the vagus nerve to our heart and activate a sensation that can help guide us to what we want most. We can engage our head-brain for greater mindfulness and self-control by asking, "What do I desire most from this situation?" When we ask, and pause to listen, we access our inner knowing. This is true awareness and power.

While we may think we are getting more done when we are moving fast, the truth is that during these times we are less clear, calm and confident. Making decisions from only our logical mind doesn't allow the unconscious knowing from our gut to manifest in full brainpower and more effective decision-making. Slowing things down to make a connection with spirit-self, we can have the self-control we need to wait for the best decision to align to our vision, values and goals.

SECTION III

Daily Lessons, Affirmations and
Challenges to Help You Stay Aligned!

Transforming from our ego-self to our spirit-self is a process of breaking mindset habits and behaviors. This doesn't happen overnight. In this section, you will get five days of daily lessons, affirmations and challenges for every 8 Spiritual Principles to help you stay aligned to your best self and your vision, values and goals!

ALIGN Principle 1—BE HUMBLE

Days 1-5

Day 1: You are but a thread among the fabric.

Many of us are confused about what it means to be humble. We think having a modest estimation of ourselves means we must put ourselves down or hide our greatness. Unfortunately, this causes those who try to be humble to often be self-effacing and unassertive. Taken to an extreme, it can also create a fear of success because we fear others will be intimidated by us or somehow reject us if we don't hold ourselves as meek and worthless. Having a feeling of insignificance or inferiority is not the definition of "humble."

To be humble is an admirable quality that not many people possess in its most helpful form. When you are humble, you can be accomplished but do not brag about it or feel superior to others. This is because your humility reminds you that it was not just you who created who you are, what you have, or what you have accomplished. There is an honest assessment of all moving parts, and people, that contributed to the result.

When we want to puff up our portion of the contribution, we have likely fallen into pride. Pride is the opposite of humility and is an over-evaluation of self, covering up a deeper insecurity that we are not enough. The most prideful people are always trying to prove themselves to others in order to get their approval. This is often seen in the form of bragging.

Humility, on the other hand, is a virtue that comes from understanding you do not get your value from others recognizing you, telling you that you are great, or having admiration for you. Someone who is truly humble has given up this need for approval because they accept their strengths and weaknesses unconditionally. People who are humble understand they are a part of a bigger force and are therefore "a thread among the fabric." When we have this modest estimation of our own individual importance and contribution, we open a space within our mindset to be humble.

Humble people share their good fortunes, but they consider these two things when they do: They share the credit with others who helped them along the way, and with God who provided their talents and blessings.

TODAY'S Affirmation:
"I am able to acknowledge others for their contribution to me."
- Susan K. Wehrley

ALIGN Challenge:
Who do you need to recognize as a contributor to you and your life?
Be sure to recognize those people this week!

Day 2: Accept yourself unconditionally, including your shortcomings.

When we're humble, yet self-accepting, we're able to embrace all facets of ourselves—not just the positive aspects we are confident others will accept. To unconditionally accept ourselves means we can recognize our weaknesses, limitations and foibles without judgment. This doesn't mean we don't want to improve our weaknesses, it just means we don't improve ourselves because of judgment. We do it out of wanting to reach our greatest potential.

If we received positive regard from our parents when we were forming our self-identities (before age eight), we are more likely to treat ourselves in this same positive regard. In contrast, if our parents were harsh and judgmental with us, we will tend to treat ourselves in the same harsh and critical way.

In other words, it's almost impossible not to treat ourselves similarly to how we were parented, unless of course we do the work of consciously deleting the scripts in our minds that don't allow us to accept ourselves. We must then replace these negative messages with new, loving messages that tell us we are enough just the way we are.

In order to be humble and more self-accepting, we need to practice self-compassion, let go of guilt, and forgive ourselves for not being what we thought we should be in order to please others. This allows us to be more authentic. By focusing more on being authentic, rather than being accepted, we begin to dissolve the shame we took on by trying to be what our parents, and everyone else, wanted us to be. By realizing it's okay for people to have biases and preferences, but that we don't need to adapt ourselves for their comfort, we begin a true love relationship with ourselves. This is a very humbling experience, as we give up the pride and shame that kept us stuck behind our own masks.

When we move forward in being and accepting our authentic selves, we begin to realize that we did more harm to ourselves, and others, when we were faking it. This is when we need to let go of the guilt and forgive ourselves for believing we needed to pretend we were someone else just to be loved and accepted. In the end, we realize there is really nothing to forgive—and that life is about unfolding our genuine self. This means recognizing and making peace with the part of ourselves we have disowned. This could be our bodies, personality traits, sexual preferences, or a characteristic about us that we judged. Until we stop splitting off segments of ourselves and become wholly who we are, it will be difficult to reach our greatest potential.

TODAY'S Affirmation:
"I am unique and accept myself unconditionally."
- Susan K. Wehrley

ALIGN Challenge:
What "shortcoming" of yours do you need to accept as perfect?

Day 3: Believe in something bigger than you.

In order to get to this humble mindset, we need to believe in something bigger than ourselves—and we must believe in the perfection of synchronicity.

Our desire to control makes us become fearful when things don't occur as we thought they should, in the timing we believe they should happen. Perhaps you found it hard to humbly accept circumstances when the following things did not occur in your life:

- *The client you wanted* so badly didn't renew their contract but later went bankrupt
(you likely wouldn't have been paid!).
- *The house you wanted to buy* but didn't get (thank goodness...you lost your job!).
- *The health condition you got* and didn't want (but later realized was the greatest catalyst to your growth in character).
- *The job you lost,* because later you discovered the perfect job was around the corner waiting for you!
- *The relationship you didn't get* (and later you were happy because you found someone better for you).
- *The employee who left* (and made you realize they were not a fit or creating results anyway).

When we believe we know what is right for us, we become attached to outcomes being what we believe they ought to be. This mindset makes us prideful, not humble.

The root cause to this prideful mindset is our inability to be vulnerable and face our fear of uncertainty. This propels us into a mindset of control instead of surrendering to the guidance of the spirit-self. On the other hand, when we are humble we accept what "is," we become curious, and we humbly ask, "How might I accept what "is" and align to what is highest and best?"

TODAY'S Affirmation:
"I am able to let go to life's perfect unfoldment."
- *Susan K. Wehrley*

ALIGN Challenge:
Where do you need to believe in something bigger than yourself and trust the unfoldment of life?

Day 4: Engage others.

We all want to receive help from time to time, but truly engaging others and allowing them to have a voice is difficult. "What if they want to do it differently than I do? What do I do if I believe their way is not the best way and therefore will not produce the best results?" These are the fears I often hear that make people want to pull up their bootstraps and do it alone, rather than humbly engaging others.

There is another way, and that is to collaborate on "how" to get to the vision. We can engage others in the "how" with the following steps in order to receive the help we need:

1) **Name a common vision:** "Don't you agree we want our home to be a place where we can feel comfortable and at peace?"
2) **Ask for their input:** "What would that look like to you? How would you believe we could achieve that vision?"
3) **After you have listened and engaged them, give your input:** "For me, my vision is a home that is more organized and cleaner. It makes me feel rested and in control. When there is mess and dirt around me, I feel chaotic inside. I think we should get some hired help to organize and clean and then set roles, responsibilities and a schedule to keep up with it."
4) **Agree to disagree:** Chart out what you first agree upon; then write down where you disagree. When you disagree, ask, "OK, how might we resolve these differences?"
5) **Create a plan of action:** Be specific. What did you agree upon? Who will do what by when? What actionable steps and strategies will help you achieve your vision? Even if you didn't make a plan and agree on everything, move forward where you do agree. It's a start!

By humbly engaging others, we feel more connected, have more support, get more buy-in and can potentially even get better ideas.

This process of engagement can be done at home or work to help people align to the vision, values and goals.

TODAY'S Affirmation:
"I am able to engage others in a vision and receive all the help I need." - Susan K. Wehrley

ALIGN Challenge:
How might you use the five steps above to do so?
Write the conversation out first so you can practice.

Day 5: Appreciate contribution.

An online study by Glassdoor revealed that more than 80 percent of employees say they're motivated to work harder when their boss is humble and shows appreciation (Chad Brooks, Business News Daily, Senior Writer, November 18, 2013). This is no different in our personal life: If you want your teenager or significant other to help you more, begin with appreciation for what they are already doing.

Feeling genuinely appreciative lifts people up. It increases their self-esteem, which helps them see their greatness in their mind's eye. As you lift people up, they have more to give and, in return, want to help. While this sounds so simple, a person must be humble to appreciate and recognize others.

When we are humble and truly grateful, we:
- **Notice people doing things right** and catch them in the moment.
- **Send thank-you notes** and are very specific about what we are thankful for.
- **Let others be a part of decision-making.** This is a form of appreciation and recognition for their talents and contributions.

Let's illustrate.
Say you have salespeople who are not hitting your goals.
You may be like Fred, who wants to hit the revenue goals but does not want to hire another person to be on the payroll. A humble leader would sit down with the salespeople and find out what they are doing. After sincerely appreciating them for their current efforts and activities, he or she would ask them, "How might we increase sales?" This contrasts with pointing out, in a critical tone, what they are doing wrong and what they need to do differently.

TODAY'S Affirmation:
"I am able to find the good in others. When I appreciate them, they always give me more help!" - Susan K. Wehrley

ALIGN Challenge:
What questions do you need to ask to get others thinking about improvement, rather than hitting them between the eyes with criticism that makes them believe they are not enough?"

ALIGN Principle 2—ASK, BELIEVE AND RECEIVE

Days 1-5

Day 1: Ask for assistance.

Many of us have been taught that asking for help or assistance is a sign of weakness. If we haven't been taught this belief, we have perhaps asked for help in the past and been disappointed from the lack of support we hoped to receive from others, or the Universe as we define it. As a result, we felt like a victim and separated from our vulnerability, pulling up our bootstraps so we could handle it on our own.

Being strong isn't bad, but getting in the habit of thinking, "If it's meant to be, it's up to me!" can cut off our ability to receive. When we cannot trust anyone else to be there for us, or do it as well as we can, we develop a grandiose E.G.O., meaning this Edges our Greatest self Out. Our "greatest self" has the ability to receive extraordinary assistance from others, and the Universe, when we do the following steps:

4 Steps to Receive Assistance
1) **Ask**: Ask very specifically, "How might I...?" Stay open to the form but specific about what you want.
2) **Seek:** Be curious and open-minded for your answer to appear!
3) **Believe:** This is the part that trips most people up. You must believe wholeheartedly in what you have asked for with complete faith and trust. You must see and feel it as though you already have it (and not yearning for it in fear you won't get it).
4) **Receive:** You must be ready to receive what you are asking for—and without doubt! Doubt slows down receiving because your chattering mind will not allow possibilities in and may not allow you to see what's right in front of you. To receive, you must maintain the state of believing.

<u>Let's illustrate:</u>
Wealthy people receive money because they are open to receiving it.
Wealthy people believe that they will always have money and therefore think of innovative ways to make more of it. What we focus on expands, and wealthy people focus on asking themselves and the Universe, "How might I receive more money?" This was a lesson for Fred, who tended to only focus on what he was not getting from his bottom-line. Fred needed to learn how not to fret about whether or not he would make money. Instead, he learned how to get excited about *how* he and his employees would receive more money. This required a paradigm shift—believing more money would come to them. This way, he could feel the joy, instead of fear, before it arrived!

TODAY'S Affirmation:
"I am able to receive abundantly when I ask and believe."
-Susan K. Wehrley

ALIGN Challenge:
Where in your life do you need to believe you can receive?

Day 2: Focus on believing.

Do you believe you deserve what you are asking for? Or does it feel like what you're yearning to receive is just outside your reach?

These are all the mindsets that get in the way of us believing we will receive what we want. When our minds don't fully believe "it" is ours, we feel self-doubt. When we feel self-doubt, our lack of confidence gets in the way of us receiving.

In order to believe we will receive what we want, we must believe we already have it—even if the facts tell us otherwise. In order to believe at this deeper level, we need to practice being in the present moment, with gratitude, and acting as if we already have what we say we want. To believe we can have more, we simply need to ask, "How might I receive more of what I already have (money, love, health, etc.)?

Let's illustrate:
You want more love.
In order to receive more love, we first must believe we have it. Instead of wishing a new relationship would come your way or someone would change, note what you currently have in the present moment. This is what Rosemary did to expand love around her and receive more of it. She looked for all the love around her. This included asking herself a few questions: Did someone glance at her with a special smile? Did someone appreciate her? Did someone go the extra mile for her to ensure she got what she asked for? Did someone reach out to her to find out how she was doing? Did someone let her know they were thinking about her? Often, we long for something that is right in front of us because we do not believe we can have what we want. What you focus on expands. Start focusing on how you already have love, and watch it expand!

TODAY'S Affirmation:
"I am able to receive abundantly when I am grateful and believe I can have more of what I already have now."
- Susan K. Wehrley

ALIGN Challenge:
Where do you need to believe you already have abundance and simply ask for more of what you already have?

Day 3: Believe in your worth.

When we don't believe we are worth what we want, no matter how clear our goals might be, we will never achieve what we say we want.

Deep within us is our greatest potential. However, while most of us could name our glowing qualities, deep within us is also our self-doubt chattering away in our minds. These are the internal messages that say, "You are not enough!" Perhaps this was never said to us directly, but it's the subtle message we tell ourselves because of someone else's critical or rejecting behavior.

A study by University of Washington researchers say that by age five, children have already formed much of their self-esteem (Molly McElroy, Institute for Learning and Brain Sciences, UW News, November 2, 2015). The problem is that by then, many of the negative messages we have given ourselves have already been stored away in our subconscious mind. As a result, they act as a set point for our comfort zone and our reactions to other people when they are triggered. When our subconscious self-doubt is triggered, we can often say or do things that are not in alignment with what we really want to create. This is because in this moment, we don't believe we can have what we want due to our self-doubt that is operating at an unconscious level.

For you to achieve new heights of success, you must be willing to do the work of digging deep down and finding the mindset messages that said to you, "I am not able to have what I want with ease!" If you don't do the work to get to these subconscious mindset messages, you cannot replace them with a new mindset that will help you believe you can get exactly what you want!

Here are four common stinkin'-thinkin' mindsets that sabotage our greatest potential:

- **Limited-thinking** causes us to be stuck and not see the possibilities before us.
- **Double-minded thinking** makes us believe we have to choose between "this or "that" and cannot have it all.
- **Deprivation-thinking** makes us believe what we want is not within our reach.
- **Self-deprecating thinking** makes us believe we are not enough.

By identifying our negative thought patterns, we can replace them with thoughts that will create the feelings, behavior and results we want!

TODAY'S Affirmation:
"I am worth receiving success and have all the talent and resources needed to get there with ease!" - Susan K. Wehrley

ALIGN Challenge:
Which of the four patterns of stinkin'-thinkin' do you get most stuck in?

Day 4: Focus on receiving by eliminating stinkin'-thinkin'.

Many of us over-value autonomy and independence and see "standing alone" as a strength. Conversely, we often judge vulnerability and dependency as weak. These misconceptions are mindsets that keep us from receiving assistance. Giving and receiving are the yin and yang in life—the natural ebb and flow when we allow it. When we don't live in this balance of ebb and flow, we give from an emptiness within ourselves (and likely from our own need to be in control or recognized). When we don't receive what we want (control and recognition), we feel resentful and exhausted. This is a sure sign we have been giving too much and not allowing ourselves to receive enough.

Unfortunately, most of us have been conditioned that receiving is far less noble than giving. We have all sorts of judgments around receiving—it's taking, selfish, needy, dependent and weak.

When we get past those judgments, we may humble ourselves enough to say, "OK, fine—I will accept your help!" But even then, purely receiving is difficult because our minds pollute the receiving with guilt, shame, criticism and fear of what we might have to do in return for our indebtedness.

In order to ALIGN to our greatest potential, we need to look at receiving through a new lens. This requires giving up our judgments and opening our mindsets to a new way of looking at receiving as a part of the natural ebb and flow of life.

Let's illustrate:
Rosemary had a difficult time asking for help, because she got her self-esteem from people-pleasing. When she didn't play the role of the "all-giver" and someone else got the job done, she struggled with messages she gave herself, such as that they were more of a team player, that they were more helpful, and that she was just being selfish. Becoming conscious of this internal dialogue and self-

doubt, Rosemary could now shift her mindset to something healthier—like, "It's great that someone else has a chance to contribute their talents, too!"

TODAY'S Affirmation:
"I am able to receive exactly what I need—
and in the perfect timing to help me reach my goals!"
- Susan K. Wehrley

ALIGN Challenge:
Where do you have stinkin'-thinkin' that is getting in your way of receiving?

Day 5: Set a vision to receive help.

A vision is an image in your mind that helps you manifest what you want. It's a picture of your will and destiny to guide you to where you need to go.

Envision something you want. Go ahead and give yourself the child-like permission to just dream. Want to build a business? Create a loving relationship? Finish a degree? Write a book? Make a million dollars? Develop real estate? Whatever it is, it begins with a vision. We are often afraid to create a vision because our mind chatters, "Right...and how is that going to work?" It is easy to fall into self-doubt and deprivation-thinking and believing we will not get what we need. Most people focus on what they can't do or what they are afraid they will not get—instead of learning how to receive help for their vision.

In order to ALIGN to your potential, you need to have a vision and receive help. When we create a powerful vision, we create a picture not only for ourselves, but for others to follow. A vision motivates people and is essential to any successful endeavor. A powerful vision is like a compass, guiding people to take the best actions to get them to the ultimate destiny. Your vision lays out a destination for others to see. Strategy, on the other hand, is "how" they will get there. By setting the vision but allowing them to be a part of the "how," you have now created ownership in the process. This level of ownership will not only raise their level of self-esteem and commitment, it will also allow you to receive help.

<u>Let's illustrate:</u>
Both Rosemary and Fred set a goal to receive more help. For Rosemary, it was in her personal life, and for Fred it was at work. Both believed they were not getting the support they desired to reach their goals. Admittedly, they both realized they had been approaching their concern in a reactive way and with criticism. This only created a power and control struggle about who was right and

who was wrong, or whose needs were more important. What both were now starting to realize is that they needed to be proactive and approach the situation from vision first. This would create cooperation, because it would ignite enthusiasm regarding why things must get accomplished. Instead of telling people what they needed to do to help, both Rosemary and Fred were not engaging others in brainstorming "how" to accomplish what must get done. This created greater buy-in and commitment because of the proactive and collaborative approach.

TODAY'S Affirmation:
"I am able to reach my potential, and receive help, when I have a vision." - Susan K. Wehrley

ALIGN Challenge:
Start with the vision instead of micro-managing "how" it will get done.

ALIGN Principle 3—FORGIVE, LET GO AND LEARN

Days 1-5

Day 1: Change your mindset: It's all perfect!

Part of aligning to our greatest potential is forgiving ourselves for not trusting that grace and synchronicity were always there to assist us.

We think forgiveness means forgiving someone else for their transgressions. What if everything was perfect, so we didn't have anything or anyone to forgive?

This is a mindset stretch that allows us to let go of a victim mentality. When we realize that everything is perfect, we can change our mindset from a victim to one that wants to learn and grow. This new mindset helps us to be with our experiences in a way that is less judgmental and more curious. By letting go of our need to be right and in control, we can be curious about where the other person is coming from, why it is what it is, and what we need to do about it to reach our greatest potential.

When we let go, we are letting go of the script in our mind that is attached to an outcome we deem it ought to be. These are the scripts we've inherited from TV, our parents, society, our churches, our community, etc. Unconsciously, we don't even realize we have a script of right and wrong, appropriate and inappropriate, good and bad. But we do! When things and people do not show up as we expect, we can be very judgmental, self-righteous, fearful and angry!

Principle 3 teaches us to forgive ourselves from taking on such scripts and projecting them onto others. Understanding this principle helps us see that we can let go of our attachment to what we want it to be. Detaching means we get curious about where that other person is coming from and how we can respond with truth and compassion rather than with a reaction.

Let's illustrate:
Your significant other has been rather crabby and negative lately. Who asked for that?! Rosemary faced this situation when she began asking for more support. She believed that all other people's significant others were more supportive than hers. Why? She saw all these posts on Facebook that made her believe so! First, Rosemary had to forgive herself for believing this illusion. Second, she had to forgive her significant other for his reactive behavior, because his belief was that women were all-supportive like his mother. When Rosemary accepted the situation as it was, and that they were in each other's lives to grow, she could let go of her judgment and learn how to be in the relationship in a more mutual way.

TODAY'S Affirmation:
"I am able let go of my expectations of others and learn what it is I need to do to create the life I want." - Susan K. Wehrley

ALIGN Challenge:
Where do you need to change your mindset and see it is all perfect??

Day 2: Forgive yourself rather than project your disappointment onto others.

When we are disappointed about the outcome of things, it is so easy to go to a place of blame in our mind. The chattering sounds a lot like, "If only they would've, could've...then I wouldn't be disappointed."

If we are not projecting this disappointment onto another person, perhaps we are projecting it onto the situation and God. Our minds chatter, "If God would've, could've...then I wouldn't be stuck here."

And finally, if we are not blaming others or God, we come back to blame ourselves: "If only I would've, could've...then I wouldn't be in this situation!" That is a futile and unproductive thought process as well.

Principle 3 teaches us how we give our power and potential away by blaming others, God, and ourselves for our circumstances. We do this because it is easier to blame than to go deeper with ourselves and ask, "How might I forgive, let go and learn?"

Admitting we are here to learn makes us feel vulnerable, whereas blaming makes us hold onto the illusion that we are in control.

By forgiving ourselves that we believed we were here to be in control, rather than learn, we open our mind to what "is" and let go of our attachments to the outcomes of safety, security, love and belonging. When we don't feel safe, secure or loved or we lack a sense of belonging, we can ask, "What do I need to let go of and learn?" This begins a journey of acceptance to what "is" as well as empowerment to what our choices are in our situation.

Let's illustrate:
if you want more revenue like Fred, instead of blaming others, yourself or God for not having more money, what if you simply

asked, "How might I forgive myself for my stronghold around money, let go of my belief I need more, and learn how to better help others with the products and service I offer?" This shift in mindset keeps us from wallowing in shame and blame, and it allows us to learn how to do things differently.

TODAY'S Affirmation:
"When things don't happen as I wish, I am able to forgive myself for projecting onto others my victim mentality." - Susan K. Wehrley

ALIGN Challenge:
Where in the last 30 days have you struggled with accepting something and asking what it is you need to learn? Do this now. What is it you need to learn so you can move forward to create the life you want?

Day 3: Let go of expectations from others, but not your dreams.

One of the lessons we need to learn is to let go of expectations from others so that we can pursue our own dreams. Letting go of others' expectations can be hard, because we have unconscious fears of being abandoned by others and not belonging to their norms. In order to make the shift to reach our potential, we need to realize this reality: The only one who can abandon us is us.

When we focus more on what others expect from us, versus what our inner guidance is leading us to do or say, we give up ourselves. No one makes us do or say anything, so the only one we need to forgive for abandoning us is us. It's true. People can expect things from us and threaten to withhold love, leave us, or be difficult if we do not give them what they want. But remember this—you have choices regarding their behavior other than abandoning yourself. This is a lesson we all need to learn in order to reach our potential.

When others' expectations do not align with your inner knowing, you can do what Rosemary learned to do—you can learn a new way of dealing with it. Try one of the following:

- **Call the bird out of the bush.**
  Say, "I notice when you don't get your way with me, you [withdraw, get mad, threaten to leave me, retaliate, etc.]. What is that about for you?" You might find out they are hurt, feel unloved and/or didn't even realize they were acting out in the way you described.
- **Observe their behavior and don't take it personally.**
  Sometimes we don't have to say anything; we can just observe someone's behavior but not make it about us. We can do this when we neutralize their behavior in our minds and say, "Hmm....isn't that interesting. I notice that they go in the other room and don't talk to me when they don't get what they want."

- **You can be vulnerable**.
    Share with them how much you want to please them and how you know you will be over-accommodating if you don't honor your inner knowing. Go into some detail as to why you know you need to choose what you do. By sharing this inner struggle, and your true reasons for not accommodating, they will begin to understand.

TODAY'S Affirmation:
"I am able to let go of others' expectations and share my "why" with them so that they don't take it personally." - *Susan K. Wehrley*

ALIGN Challenge:
When have you heard others' expectations and called the bird out of the bush, observed their behavior, or been vulnerable without feeling the need to please them?
How might you practice doing that in your life now?

Day 4: Learn when you are playing the victim and giving your power away.

We know we have learned the lesson that we own our power when we stop playing the victim. Playing the victim means you see others and situations as somehow having power over you, your success, happiness, safety, security, well-being, etc.

You know you are in your power and not playing the victim when you can witness happenings as things that just happen. You can learn to do this by saying to yourself, "Hmmm....isn't that interesting. [This] just happened."

This neutralizes the emotion we have about a situation and makes us curious instead of anxious or angry. Observing and becoming more curious are the characteristics of a person who has come into their power. Nothing stirs them up and gets them anxious and angry. This is because they hold a deep belief of:

"This or something better is coming my way!"

By having the belief that life looks out for you and that things are always unfolding to perfection, you don't have to dramatize situations or actions of others. When you don't like the way things are going, ask yourself:

"How might I make this work out for me?"

Because you are in your power, you do what you must do to make things work out. You let go of what others think and do not manage your image. You also do not get caught up in fear-based thinking, wondering how you could get hurt if you do and say what is right for you. You let go of any fearful imaginings and do what you know you need to do.

Let's illustrate:

You just lost your best salesperson because they went to work for the competition.

This is the fear many business owners, like Fred, have when holding employees accountable. Sure, there would be a moment of feeling shocked and betrayed if this was the result. But the person with power would take a deep breath and say to him/herself, "This or something better is on its way. Life always works out for me. This person was with me for the perfect amount of time, and now something even better will appear. Time to move on!" Those in a victim mindset would be telling everyone their woe story. The person who can forgive, let go and learn stays in their power and moves forward.

TODAY'S Affirmation:
"I am at peace because life always works out for me."
- Susan K. Wehrley

ALIGN Challenge:
What do you need to forgive, let go of and learn so you can stay in your power?

Day 5: Take responsibility for creating what you want.

It's so much easier to blame than to take responsibility. Why is that? It is because we tend to see ourselves through the lens of our E.G.O., which Edges our Greatest self Out.

When we look through the lens of our spirit-self instead, we see how powerful we really are in co-creating the life we want. This is the lesson we need to learn, which includes taking responsibility. What gets in the way of us taking responsibility is the childlike mindset in us that causes a victim mentality.

When we see the power to create the life we want outside of ourselves, we have a small locus of control. This means we see everyone and everything else as holding the key to what we want.

This is what children do: They see the authority outside of themselves and then feel like a victim when they can't get what they want. Unfortunately, in American society, we do not do a great job of taking children through a passageway to adulthood. We pay for their college educations, their weddings, and often continue to give them money and advice to bring them comfort. At some point, there needs to be a letting go—allowing our children to live their own lives and make their own mistakes. When we do this, we teach them how to figure it out and rely on their inner guidance to help them lead the way. When we don't do this, we make them believe the answers and power are outside of themselves. This lack of responsibility mindset gets projected onto all kinds of people and situations.

Let's illustrate:
Your significant other is not giving you the love you want.
Rosemary was learning, like you can, that letting go of the need to control her boyfriend's reaction is an act of love. This also gives her the permission to be authentic and do the same. In times like this when we feel disconnected to others, we can take responsibility for

tending to our own needs. This may mean doing deeper work to see what it is you really want in a relationship—or perhaps using this time to take care of yourself physically or do that project you've always wanted to do. The key is to broaden your locus of control, forgive yourself for believing someone else has the key to love you, let go of your attachment to needing love from someone else, and learn how to cultivate self-love and loving relationships with yourself and others.

TODAY'S Affirmation:
"I am able to make the changes I need to make in order to have the life I want."- Susan K. Wehrley

ALIGN Challenge:
Where have you taken responsibility in the last month for something you really wanted, instead of hoping someone else would change or fix it for you?

ALIGN Principle 4—STAY OPEN-MINDED AND GET CURIOUS

Days 1-5

Day 1: You have plenty of time, so stop rushing.

According to brain research, open-mindedness is a function of our brain anatomy. Let me explain: Everything begins with a thought, which activates our mind. One closed-minded thought that many of us share is, "I don't have enough time!" As a result, most of us run around to get the things done, like chickens with our heads cut off. We act as though everything we are doing is urgent and important. First, most of these things are not as urgent or important as we deem. Second, this thought sends us into a closed-minded state of being—one that causes us to rush, breathe rapidly and disconnect from our gut.

When we rush and breathe in a shallow way, we change our brainwaves from alpha to beta. This puts us in a state of consciousness that is very narrow and focused on the task at hand. While this task may get done more rapidly, we are missing many of the cues at the tip of the iceberg that are telling us to yield, stop, and proceed with caution. It is difficult to be open-minded and trust our gut when we are so singularly focused and not paying attention to things, people and possibilities around us.

<u>Let's illustrate:</u>
Imagine two drivers on the highway. One is going 65 miles an hour, while the other is going 100 miles an hour. In both cars, there is a woman passenger in labor who needs to get to the hospital. In the first car, the driver is thinking, "I have plenty of time to get to the hospital. I will drive deliberately and with awareness." The second driver is thinking, "Oh no...she is in labor! I hope I have enough time to get to the hospital before she has this baby!" There is a police car on the side of the road up by the bridge, which is just around the corner. Who do you think is more likely to see the police car— the one going 65 miles an hour, who is driving deliberately with an open-mind, or the one going 100 miles an hour, who is fearful they will not get to the hospital on time? The one going 100 miles an hour will get pulled over and delayed getting to the hospital, while

the other will get there on time with less stress.

When we breathe into our gut, focus on our intention and keep an open mindset, we achieve our goals with more ease. This is because brain researchers have identified there is a "brain" in our gut. When we breathe deeply into our gut, we activate neurotransmitters and neurons that send a signal to the brain that alerts us to signals and possibilities we need to know in order to be more effective. When we are rushing and not breathing in our gut, we miss this mind-gut connection and the information that would otherwise help us reach our potential.

TODAY'S Affirmation:
"I am able to stay open-minded and trust my gut."
- Susan K. Wehrley

ALIGN Challenge:
Where in your life do you need to believe you have enough time—and therefore stop rushing?

Day 2: There is a difference between the chatterbox and the still-small voice.

When we begin to slow down and breathe, we automatically eliminate the chatterbox of fearful thoughts in our mind. When we breathe deeply, we change this brainwave from alpha to beta.

The chatterbox in our mind is our anxiety, constantly reminding us of everything we must do, not forget, be concerned about, etc. This keeps us uptight and desiring to control everything around us so that we don't have to feel our fear. This is a very different state of being than when we are fully connected to our mind, heart and gut. Through deep breathing, we get in sync with our higher self— that connection that occurs when our brainwave, heart wave and gut are in tune with each other via the vagus nerve.

Unless we are breathing deeply and slowing down, this connection cannot occur. When we are not connected fully in this way and are only operating from our head-brain, we can be sure the chatterbox of anxiety is controlling our lives. This is because subconsciously, our mind knows we are not listening to the subtle cues of our gut. As a result, the mind "screams" at us to get us to slow down and pay attention—like a child who wants us to know their needs! Here is how we can discern the voices:

The chatterbox has a hard-pressing tone in our mind that tell us, "If it is meant to be, it's up to me!" "You must do this NOW!" This voice is harsh and puts pressure on us.

The still-small voice, on the other hand, sees the situation and concern but guides us on what to do in a clear, calm and confident way.

Let's illustrate:
You have a half hour to get a project done at work.
In the past, Rosemary would have faced this situation and asked

herself, "How am I going to get this done?!" At that moment, her mind would begin to chatter and send her into anxiety, even if she tried hard to control the situation. With a few deep breaths, she now says to herself, "I have all the time I need to get this done. How might I engage others in supporting me?" Suddenly she has access to increased Gut Intelligence, and the still-small voice within tells her to ask her team member if she can have more time to finish.

TODAY'S Affirmation:
"I am able to hear the still-small voice when I breathe deeply and slow down." - Susan K. Wehrley

ALIGN Challenge:
Think of a time you listened to the still-small voice (instead of the chatter box). What were the benefits?

Day 3: Eliminate fear by connecting to your Gut Intelligence.

As you have learned, it is important to use your deep breath to bypass any unconscious fears, especially those that send you into a fight or flight response. It is this fight or flight pattern that gets you stuck in your head, trying to manage the things you wish you could control. While you may not consciously be experiencing the feeling of fear, you know you are in fear when you attempt to control the outcome.

Conversely, you know you are clear, calm and confident when you instead choose to S.T.O.P. before reacting. Here is how the S.T.O.P. technique helps you activate your vagus nerve so you can connect your gut, heart and head-brain—and be more clear, calm and confident.

S - Slow down and breathe deeply
Start at the chest, and breathe into it three times. Then take three slow breaths to the top of your belly. Then three more deep breaths to the middle of your belly.

T - Tune in within
Now ask yourself, "How might I...?" What is the problem you want to solve?

O - Observe what your intuition is telling you
Heighten your awareness to what is happening around you. What are the facts?

P - Perceive a new possibility
Ask, "How might we handle this situation so we can stay aligned to our best selves and our vision, values and goals?"

While you may think you don't have time to do the S.T.O.P. technique, with practice, this technique can be done in less than 60 seconds. The first couple of times you do it, don't be surprised if you do not get any guidance from your intuition to make you feel more clear, calm and confident. Like everything, practice makes perfect!

Let's illustrate:

Someone is going in a direction you believe will not yield the desired results.

This has happened to Fred in the past, but he didn't step in proactively. Now he does—by slowing down to breathe, tuning in to what he wants, observing the details, and engaging his employees in the problem-solving question, **"How might we handle this situation so that we stay aligned to our best selves and our vision, values and goals?"**

TODAY'S Affirmation:
"I am able to stay open-minded and trust my gut."
- Susan K. Wehrley

ALIGN Challenge:
Think of a situation within the last few months when slowing down and tuning into your gut-knowing helped you become more clear, calm and confident.

Practice the S.T.O.P. technique when you need guidance.

Day 4: Trust your Gut Intelligence even when it feels uncomfortable.

Once you begin to open your mind and trust yourself, you realize that you are living at a different level of consciousness than most other people.

This can make you feel alone (and sometimes kind of crazy), because others perceive a different reality than you. When this happens, it's tempting to go back to living in denial—where you can belong to group-think. You know the scenario: The elephant in the room is obvious, but others are walking around it in denial. You wonder, "Really...am I the only one who sees such an obvious thing?"

The Emperor's New Clothes is a great illustration of this phenomena. It shows us how people are attached to seeing things as they want to for their own safety, security, love and belonging. In the play, when the king's people announce he is wearing a beautiful garment (even though he is standing on the stage in his underwear), people deny their gut-knowing and applaud—except for the little boy in the audience who shouts that he's in his underwear! Of course, the boy gets scorned for this "disobedience" and is taught to not honor his own gut-knowing or he will be chastised or deemed crazy.

Trusting your Gut Intelligence when others are not seeing the elephant in the room can feel scary. The reason we don't trust our gut (even though deep down we know), is because we are attached to one of the following outcomes, according to Maslow:
- **Safety and security** - We are afraid if we see the truth and confront it, we may endanger our financial, physical or emotional security.
- **Love and belonging** - We would rather prescribe to group-think and think like others than be criticized or chastised for being different.

Let's illustrate:

The company you work for is telling you they are financially secure, yet they are making cut-backs on everything and you are hearing bill collectors call.

You ask your boss if the company is secure, and you are told, "We are doing great. You have nothing to worry about!" Do you believe these words, or are you paying attention to the pieces of the puzzle your gut is picking up? If you are like Rosemary, you will believe your gut—and you'll start looking for another job.

TODAY'S Affirmation:
"When I listen to my gut, I am able to trust myself instead of what others tell me."- Susan K. Wehrley

ALIGN Challenge:
Think of a time you didn't trust your gut. Did you see later, in hindsight, that you should have? What were you attached to—safety and security, or love and belonging?

Day 5: Stay in the mindset of wonder.

Having a mindset of wonder is a different way to engage with our brains, and it's not something most people do. Most people affix on a situation or person, get an attached perspective, and then angst over it.

What if you opened your mind before dropping to the bottom-line and just wondered? Wonder allows us a heightened consciousness because we don't make quick conclusions or judgments. It takes training to keep the mind open and just wonder.

When we wonder, we become curious. Curiosity is a state of mind where we want to learn more. It gives us the urge to explore before jumping to conclusions. When we are curious, we are more vigilant to gain knowledge.

If you were like many children, you likely drove your parents crazy because at one time you were extremely curious. I bet your favorite word was, "Why?" Parents who are overwhelmed will often unconsciously shut their children's curiosity down by becoming short and impatient when they ask too many questions.

Leaders and people in our personal lives can do this too—especially if we are becoming curious about something they don't necessarily want to discuss. As a result, we are aware of the ramifications of curiosity: It can make others feel uncomfortable.

But what if you just observed that reality and stayed in the mindset of wonder anyway? Imagine how much more you would know.

Let's illustrate:
Fred noticed the week's sales were down. Instead of getting upset or waiting until the end of the month, he got curious. When he asked specific questions as to "why" this was happening, his

employees became uncomfortable because Fred was holding them accountable with his curiosity. Instead of shutting his curiosity down, he just observed their reactions and kept asking questions. Finally, Fred got to the root cause that he could now solve.

TODAY'S Affirmation:
"I am able to trust my Gut Intelligence to alert me when I need to step in and get curious."- Susan K. Wehrley

ALIGN Challenge:
Think of a time you would have benefited by stepping in and getting curious.

ALIGN Principle 5—PRACTICE GRATITUDE

Days 1-5

Day 1: Detach from the outcomes.

Practicing gratitude is an art. The thing is, people are not hardwired to be grateful, because they can become affixed to what they think they deserve or "should" be receiving. This can be anything from a sunny day to flowers on Valentine's Day.

We have an automatic fight/flight response when life and people do not show up as we expected. This is because all our experiences first must pass through the lower part of the brain, which is hardwired for judging our experiences as "good" or "bad." This gets us looking out for danger and disappointment, making it difficult to automatically see what is working versus what is not.

Fight-flight responses make us believe there is a big bear around the corner about to eat us up, when in fact it is just a little mouse that got in the house and can be easily trapped. It still might not be ideal, but when you are practicing gratitude, you don't focus on the mouse in the house or the worst that can happen. Did they also let in the big bad bear? No! We are just grateful we have a house, that it is just a mouse, and that someone created peanut butter and mousetraps (or exterminators and a phone so you can call them). No big deal!

Within our lessons on gratitude, you will learn how not to waste your mind-energy on disappointment and frustration when things do not go exactly as you expected. Instead, you will be grateful because you will look for the secret blessing in it all. This will give you a new perspective, knowing life is unfolding perfectly. By looking at what life is presenting to you in a different perspective, you begin to appreciate, with gratitude, all that occurs. Even the difficult lessons and situations you will begin to understand were designed to lead you to your greater potential. Because you have developed the quality of being grateful, you benefit because you now see situations in the right perspective and realize what you have is just perfect.

Because we understand that "what we focus on expands," we know that focusing on gratitude expands our happiness. This is not being Pollyanna-positive—it is choosing to look at what is working in our life, instead of what is not working, and moving forward.

TODAY'S Affirmation:
"I am focusing, with gratitude, on what is working in my life."
- Susan K. Wehrley

ALIGN Challenge:
Think of a situation where you focused on the negative right away, rather than first focusing on the positive and being grateful. Then, simply shift your mindset and focus on gratitude.
How did that make you feel?

Day 2: Breathe past fear, and connect with gratitude.

I love James Bond movies. Why? They remind me of how taking a deep breath in the face of adversity makes us feel: confident and grateful. I always wondered why James Bond relaxed before a big confrontation—until I learned the brain science research that explained how this phenomenon of breathing works.

Most of us breathe in a shallow way all day long. The shallower we breathe, the more stressed we get because we get caught up in the lower part of our brain that puts us in the fight-flight response that makes us panic. As we learn to breathe and "whistle while we work," we are filled with greater gratitude naturally, because we feel deep down like we are a human *being*—, not a human *doing*. You might be thinking, "Yeah right...you don't have five kids like I do, or a demanding job like mine." You might be right; however, no matter what responsibilities or obstacles are before you, breathing deeply will allow you to get out of the fight-flight part of your brain and soar to new heights of thinking and being. Instead of working hard, you will be working smart—and full of pep in your step—when you breathe deeply.

This takes you beyond the type of gratitude that is merely saying "thank you" more often. It is the type of gratitude you feel when you breathe deeply into your life and body. Through the power of your breath, your mindfulness shifts to one that is focused on the here and now. This leaves no room for your mind to wander into the past and regret decisions. It also leaves no room to rush ahead into the future, worrying about if something may or may not work out as you think it should. Instead, you are right in the here and now, slowing things down through your breath and taking in all that "is" with gratitude. Slowing down and breathing helps us to savor the moments in life.

When we are frightened or stressed, the limbic system in our brain is shouting at our frontal lobe and the rest of our body, saying,

"Hey! We are in a crisis here!" The logical part of our brain believes the limbic system, and our whole body begins to respond with shallow breaths. Our blood pressure increases, and our body tenses up. If we discover we are safe, we let out a deep breath, and our equilibrium is restored. By breathing deeply and focusing on gratitude, we are short-cutting the stress process, going directly to a stress-free experience. Not only is this a healthier way to live, but we are able to tap into our greater potential because we are operating at a higher awareness.

TODAY'S Affirmation:
"It is what it is. I am able to breathe deeply, with gratitude, that this isn't a catastrophic issue. Life always works out for me!"
- Susan K. Wehrley

ALIGN Challenge:
Think of a time in the last week when you faced a difficult situation and were stressed. Now pretend you are in the moment again.
Start breathing deeply.
Ask yourself, "What can I be grateful for?"

Day 3: Change your schema.

We all have a filter in our brain called a "schema" that filters information in a way that is meaningful for us. It's a pattern and thought process that allows us to create a framework and mental structure for our preconceived ideas.

Within our schema is a tendency for self-protection. As a result, we quickly scan information, and if there is any preconceived notion that a change may create danger or deprivation for us, we automatically react in a fight-flight pattern. This schema acts as protection to keep us from being hurt, abandoned, betrayed or disappointed. While that might sound good in some ways, it is also a detriment to our ability to reach our full potential because when our schema is causing us to play defense, we are not playing offense.

It is near to impossible to reach our full potential and our goals when we are self-protective and playing defense. In order to change our schema, we must first change our habit by exercising a new way of being. This means we need to train our mind to look for what is working and how to make that work even better. Notice how we are training our mind to start from abundance. What we focus on expands; therefore, being grateful for the abundance that "is" will create more abundance. When we train our mind to think in this abundant and grateful way, our schema changes. Pretty soon, it becomes a habit to see what is working and to be grateful for it, versus seeing what is not working and to be fearful and agitated. Great leaders understand the practice of changing their schema, as do great parents and partners.

Let's illustrate:
It's raining outside. What do you see?
How often do you hear people complain about the weather? I find it interesting that people would allow the weather to ruin their mood and day. If you are like Rosemary, you admit you get caught

up in this group-think! When it is raining outside, instead of being grateful the flowers are getting watered, it is easy to complain that you can't go for a walk. Imagine how much happier you would be if you could be grateful for the little ways life really is supporting you!

TODAY'S Affirmation:
"I am able to find something to be grateful for in every situation, before I begin process improvements." - Susan K. Wehrley

ALIGN Challenge:
Where do you need to stop focusing on the negative and begin to first see the positive?

Day 4: Learn to compliment others.

Why do we find it so difficult to compliment others? When I ask people this question, I often hear the following:
- It makes people feel uncomfortable.
- The people they compliment may get too full of themselves.
- The people they compliment will take them for granted.
- Others will then have the upper hand.
- Eventually, those I compliment will see themselves as better than I am (and so will I).
- It makes me feel vulnerable.

When we compliment others, we are saying to them, "I notice and appreciate you!" Complimenting is an act of gratitude. Whether that is someone's personality, talents, ideas, new outfit, haircut or something they did to go the extra mile, we are demonstrating our ability to be conscious, aware and grateful. It shows more about our ability to be grateful than anything about them.

However, for some, giving compliments is uncomfortable and creates anxiety. Here are a few tips to become better at giving compliments: Be sincere, respectful, specific, focused on things they value, and uplifting. When we exercise this muscle in our mind and compliment others, we become more grateful in life by allowing others to feel important and appreciated.

Let's illustrate:
Your significant other cleaned the kitchen, but not the way you would have done it. How do you compliment him sincerely?
Oh, Rosemary struggled with this one! When she saw the pots and pans sitting in the sink (drying, but not put away), she raised her eyebrows and felt critical. She didn't say a word, but she wanted to say, "Couldn't you just have finished the job?!" Then she remembered it was her choice to see what she wanted to see. So, she noticed he unloaded the dishwasher, cleaned the refrigerator, wiped the floor, took out the garbage, and cleaned the top of the

stove. As a result of this positive focus, she felt grateful and instead said, "Wow! The kitchen really looks clean. I can see how you unloaded the dishwasher, cleaned the refrigerator, wiped the floor, took out the garbage, and cleaned the top of the stove. Thank you!"

TODAY'S Affirmation:
"I am able to see people doing things right, and I compliment them freely. Complimenting others makes both of us feel good."
- Susan K. Wehrley

ALIGN Challenge:
Think of a situation in the last week where you could have complimented someone more. Who was it, and what would you have said?

Day 5: Be grateful for your uniqueness.

One of the greatest lessons we can learn is to not compare ourselves to each other. Unfortunately, we are taught to do so by society and many parents. Women tend to compare themselves to other women when it comes to their beauty, relationships, homes and children. Men often compare themselves to other men when it comes to how smart they are, their accomplishments, wealth, physical strength, and the beautiful woman on their arm.

Just as our minds can get conditioned to compare ourselves to others, we can also condition our minds to be grateful for our uniqueness. One of the most important aspects of becoming your full potential is learning to be grateful for who you are instead of comparing yourself to others.

This requires us to take an inventory of how we were uniquely made and how that may have lined up perfectly to our vision.

Let's illustrate:
You think someone has a quality better than you.
It wasn't until Fred did an inventory of his uniqueness that he could see he didn't have to be the exact same kind of leader as his dad. His natural personality was more laid back, and his peace came from spending time outside with animals. When Fred took his uniqueness into account and appreciated it rather than compared it to his dad, he could see how he could create a unique work culture based on mindfulness and engagement. This made Fred feel great, as he could do his job as president and CEO in a way that was aligned to his true self. Not only did this change his style of communication, it changed some policies at work—such as allowing employees to bring their pets to work. Since Fred loved animals so much, he offered "pet care" along with "day care" to help employees balance their lives. Fred was appreciating his uniqueness and finding ways to celebrate it in his life!

TODAY'S Affirmation:
"I am able to appreciate my uniqueness as perfect for my purpose in life."- Susan K. Wehrley

ALIGN Challenge:
Think of a situation where you can stop comparing yourself to others and appreciate your uniqueness now.

ALIGN Principle 6—EMBRACE GRACE AND SYNCHRONICITY

Days 1-5

Day 1: Step into the unknown.

Being in the present moment allows you to move through life effortlessly. You are no longer wasting energy thinking about the past or worrying about the future. You are trusting your spirit-self and the simultaneous occurrences of events that appear to have no discernible causal connection.

This state of awareness has always existed—it's just that now you have heightened awareness and have learned to acknowledge grace and synchronicity! In the past, because you operated more often from your E.G.O. (Edging your Greatest self Out), you believed "I" did this and that.

When you experience synchronicity, you experience situations like:
- Thinking about a person you haven't spoken to in a long time and then running into them at the grocery store.
- Deciding to take a detour and then finding out you missed an accident on the route you would have otherwise taken.
- Sitting down next to someone who happens to have the perfect job, house or referral (whatever you have been asking for!).

There is a popular passage from the Bible that has become mainstream: "By the Grace of God go I!" This saying acknowledges that most people realize something bigger than us is at play.

The whole concept of grace and synchronicity originated from Carl Jung, who invented the term to describe the alignment of "universal forces" with the life experiences of an individual. Jung's principle emphasizes the power of our thoughts to attract us to what we want to create. While most of us believe the concept of the book *The Secret* is new, it is actually biblically based and was made popular by Jung's work.

Now that you see grace and synchronicity for what they are, you step into the ability to co-partner with this force at work in your life. As a result, you embrace this partnership along the path of your success. Having such assistance makes you lighter and less burdened along the way! The belief that "success takes a lot of work" or "If it's meant to be, it's up to me!" is now deleted from your belief system.

TODAY'S Affirmation:
"I am able to tap into grace and synchronicity by letting go of my E.G.O. that wants to Edge my Greatest self Out!" - Susan K. Wehrley

ALIGN Challenge:
Where do you need to be in the present moment so that you can see how grace and synchronicity want to help you?

Day 2: Let go of your need to control.

When we let go of our need to control, we are suddenly on the same wavelength as grace and synchronicity. It's as though life is a radio station, and we have to be tuned into the right channel to receive the messaging.

When we are tuned into the frequency of our E.G.O. (Edging our Greatest self Out), we cannot receive grace and synchronicity because we are in the wavelength of, "If it's meant to be, it's up to me!" Our mind is chattering so loud that we cannot hear grace and synchronicity speaking to us or showing us the way. Even if grace and synchronicity are trying to help us out, we will have our earplugs in and blinders on—so we don't hear the calling or see the easiest path of least resistance.

From a young age, we are taught to try to control the outcomes of things others deem important. We were taught to make sure we have things under control, like:
- Our appearance
- Our manners
- Our bedroom
- Our chores
- Our grades
- Our behavior
- Our "appropriate" choices

Because we have learned to try to control these outcomes and impressions, we get an unconscious feeling of shame when we don't meet our "control list." This can lead to being overwhelmed, anxious and eventually depressed. To avoid this downward spiral, many people try to control their world instead of learning to let go of the need to control such outcomes (and get in the flow of grace and synchronicity).

It can be tricky to learn how to reach our greatest potential while giving up control. This seems at the surface like a dichotomy. However, living our greatest potential does not mean striving and driving. Instead, it means living by inspired action instead of perspired action. In order to get in step with grace and synchronicity, we need to cultivate our ability to be more open, trusting and allowing—instead of living in fear, judgment and control.

TODAY'S Affirmation:
"I am able to open my mind, trust, and allow grace and synchronicity in my life!"- *Susan K. Wehrley*

ALIGN Challenge:
Think of a situation where you want to be more open, trusting and allowing versus living by fear, judgment and control. As Nike says, "Just do it!"

Day 3: Create your thoughts.

Our thoughts are powerful. We create our thoughts, so be careful what you think about—what you think about, you will bring about!

So where do our thoughts come from? Our unconscious mind stores our beliefs, and our thoughts stem from these beliefs. Because we are not often conscious of our beliefs, we can also be unconscious of our thoughts. Pretty soon, these beliefs and thoughts take on a life of their own in our mind. As a result, we are feeling a certain way and operating according to these thoughts and beliefs without even knowing it.

Imagine you chose to be more conscious of your thoughts throughout the day. What if you were the one to decide what you thought and therefore what you felt? This puts the responsibility back on you to co-create what you want in your life with grace and synchronicity. Your thoughts let God and the Universe know what you believe you deserve.

For example, what if you lost a lot of money, for one reason or another—bad investment, a breakup, or you lost your job. Your belief might be, "I won't be able to replace that money because [fill in your belief]." Your belief could be your age, lack of opportunities, how long you took to earn it, bad economy, etc.

You can see how intertwined thoughts and beliefs are and that it's hard to distinguish one from the other. Now imagine what you would feel from this belief and thought. Not good, right? Because you know your thoughts are powerful, you can decide to choose what to think.

Let's illustrate:
Your pet got out of the house and is lost.
You could believe a lot of things from this one, such as: You will never find them, they are dead, scared or hurt, they will starve,

someone will steal them, or they will never find their way back home. Imagine what those thoughts would make you feel and how you would behave! While all those things could be true, why would you think the worst possible thoughts? You could instead think, "That little rascal needed an adventure, I guess. Good for him. I am sure he is having lots of fun meeting friends around the neighborhood and will return safe and sound soon! I'll just call a few neighbors in the meantime to make sure they keep a lookout!"

TODAY'S Affirmation:
"I am able to consciously choose my thoughts in alignment with how I want grace and synchronicity to assist me."
- Susan K. Wehrley

ALIGN Challenge:
When in the last month have you let your negative thoughts rule your mind?
How did this keep you from being able to receive grace and synchronicity?

Day 4: Waiting in the unknown builds discernment.

What does it mean to be discerning? Discernment is having the ability to make good decisions in alignment with divine will. It is the ability to see beyond our fleshly desires so that we have the ability to see the truth and obtain understanding of what direction to take.

Discernment is the ability to obtain clear perceptions and to judge a situation or person correctly. It's wisdom that often comes to us as we patiently wait for grace and synchronicity to reveal themselves to us. Consequently, if you are aware of something you are curious about and ask your spirit-self to reveal truth to you, you will get a sign that makes sense to you. This may not happen in seconds, minutes, hours, or even days. But when it does happen, you get chills up your spine and that "a-ha" knowing—a heightened awareness that gives you the discernment you asked to receive.

Discernment is listening to:
- The signs the Universe gives you to answer your question.
- That still-small voice that whispers in your ear.
- A gut alert that is followed by increased Gut Intelligence to help you align to your vision, values and goals.
- The Fruit of the Spirit that gives you a feeling of love, joy, peace, patience, kindness, goodness, faithfulness, gentleness and self-control.

<u>Let's illustrate:</u>
Someone you care about has withdrawn.
To have discernment is to see the situation for what it is, not what you want it to be. The fact is, they have withdrawn. You can make up stories in your mind as to *why* they are withdrawing. On the negative side, you might think they don't love you anymore, they are having an affair, they lost interest, they are boring, they are getting terminally sick, etc. Or you can make up a positive story that denies what is occurring and tell yourself, "Maybe they are not

really withdrawing...maybe it's my imagination." Discernment allows you to tap into grace and synchronicity to answer your question, "Why are they withdrawing?" Perhaps you asked, and they deny it, but your gut knows differently. Now grace and synchronicity answer your question when you accidently see an upsetting email they received the same day the behavior started to occur. Your inner voice tells you, "They have withdrawn because they don't know how to tell you this!" Before doing anything, you meditate on it and wait for an answer about how to approach them.

TODAY'S Affirmation:
"I am able to be discerning when I let go of my attachments to the outcome!"- Susan K. Wehrley

ALIGN Challenge:
Think of a situation where you now want to be more discerning. What attachments do you need to let go of to hear discernment?

Day 5: Follow through with your part of the partnership.

Now that we have cultivated our ability to discern, we need to follow through on what we know we need to do or say. Sounds simple, right? Not really. Discernment is one aspect of getting in the flow of grace and synchronicity. Following through means we trust that we heard the calling and will be obedient to execute what we know we need to do or say.

Why is this so difficult for us? Let's admit it: By nature, we love instant gratification—and we love to be in control. Yes, all of us. People who are highly motivated by power, prestige and money have learned to do what they need to do to reach their goals and tend to think in terms of immediate rewards. This makes it difficult to delay gratification and focus more on discernment and future rewards.

For example, can you relate to any of these examples where your instant gratification kept you from being discerning and following through with what you said you wanted most?

- You want a loving relationship, but you want to be selfish and do what you want this weekend.
- You want to save money, but you want to go shopping whenever you want.
- You want to engage others in solving the problem, but you want to just get it done and do it your way.

Let's illustrate:
You want to lose weight.
You may say you want to lose weight, and discernment tells you this when you go to your doctor and see the numbers on the scale. But while you envision what you want for yourself, you tend to want the instant gratification of eating that ice cream or brownie right now! Then later, you feel ashamed of yourself because you did not follow through with your discernment.

Understanding why we chose instant gratification and didn't follow through will help you choose differently next time. Studies have shown that anticipation of a reward activates a chemical in our brain called dopamine. This is a pleasure hormone that becomes addictive to us. When we have encoded a habit formation in our brain such as eating when we are frustrated or sad, our unconscious mind takes us to the refrigerator every time these feelings come up. In order to change this instant gratification, we need to first recognize the current stimulus pattern and then replace it with something more discerning.

TODAY'S Affirmation:
"I am able to delay gratification, follow through and reach my goals."- Susan K. Wehrley

ALIGN Challenge:
In what area of your life do you know you need to follow through with discernment?
What is the gratification you do not want to delay?

ALIGN Principle 7—FOCUS ON YOUR VISION AND DESIRE

Days 1-5

Day 1: Focus on what you want, not what you don't want.

Now that you are becoming free of the fear-chattering in your mind, you can focus more on what you want. In the past, you may have focused more on "not goals," which tell us what we don't want—such as:
- I do not want my expenses to exceed my revenue.
- I do not want to have to do it all myself.
- I do not want to have to think of everyone else's needs.
- I do not want to have a job I do not love.

When we are not in alignment with our vision and desires, we often speak in terms of what it is we do not want. This is because we received a gut alert that something was off. The above, spoken in terms of vision and desires, would sound like:
- I want more revenue than expenses.
- I want others to pitch in.
- I want mutual relationships.
- I want a job I love.

After we have made these clear claims regarding what we want, we can focus on our vision and desires by asking our spirit-self to guide us in getting there. To increase our Gut Intelligence, we must learn how to articulate what it is we envision and desire and ask, "How might I get it?"

Focusing on your vision and desires by tuning into what you want and engaging your spirit-self, will bring solutions to you through ideas, grace and synchronicity.

Let's illustrate:
Instead of Fred getting frustrated that he was stuck in traffic and potentially going to be late for his manager meeting, Fred focused on what he wanted: He wanted to start the meeting on time. He called into the office and asked the receptionist to connect him into the conference room so he could start the meeting while driving.

To keep being effective and yet be safe driving, he suggested they flip the schedule and let the manager reports go first. Where Fred would normally have been frustrated and late for his meeting, he proactively demonstrated how he stayed aligned to his vision and desires, regardless of obstacles.

TODAY'S Affirmation:
"I can make the most of every moment and ALIGN to my vision and desires!"
- Susan K. Wehrley

ALIGN Challenge:
In what circumstances do you need to stop focusing on what you aren't getting
and begin to focus on how to create your vision and desires?

Day 2: Learn how your pain is prompting your purpose.

The beauty of hindsight is that we can often see why things occurred in our lives. While some of these occurrences were painful, they often brought us to our purpose. Many of us may not know our purpose consciously—only our soul knows our purpose. We can find our purpose by following our pain. What did we not want in our lives that occurred? Ask your spirit-self, "How might this pain be prompting my purpose?"

I can think of dozens of times where someone told me they:
- ***Lost a loved one*** and then created a movement as a result (ex: the breast cancer awareness program—the founder lost her sister).
- ***Lost their job*** and then started the business they loved (ex: Steve Jobs was fired from his job...thank goodness...I love my iPhone!).
- ***Lost the marriage they were in*** and found the love of their life (This happened to a neighbor of mine who lost her husband in 9/11 and was then reconciled with her high school boyfriend).
- ***Had a child who was sick so they quit their job*** and later started their own business to have more flexibility in their life (This was my story! My daughter is perfectly healthy now...but aren't you glad this happened, or we wouldn't have met!).

While we would never wish for someone to die, lose a job or be sick, understand your vision and values are leading you to your purpose. This requires us to let go of fear, be open-minded, and wonder how this pain may be prompting our purpose. It doesn't mean you won't have feelings. Feelings are just energy that help us work through grief so that we can navigate towards our purpose. These emotions help us change out of our victim mentality, through our pain, and to our purpose. Here are some examples of emotions and what they are telling us:

- **Fear:** Being scared is a form of fear. Ask yourself, "What am I afraid will happen? How might this situation be showing me my purpose?"
- **Disappointment:** Being disappointed is a recognition that things didn't turn out as you hoped. To find your purpose, ask, "How might I use this disappointment to create greater fulfillment for myself and others?"
- **Anger:** Anger (or frustration) is an emotion that says, "Something needs to change!" Get open-minded and curious to find out what that is.
- **Sadness:** Sadness tells us we lost something or someone. Get curious: What do you miss most?

TODAY'S Affirmation:
"I am aligned to my vision. Even my pain is leading me to my purpose!" - Susan K. Wehrley

ALIGN Challenge:
Looking back at the last 60 days, where could you have turned your pain into purpose?

Day 3: Learn how your passion leads you to your purpose.

As we learn to listen to the wisdom of our emotions, we realize that not only does our pain lead to our purpose, but so does our passion.

You know when you are doing something that makes you feel complete and joyous because you feel lighter and happier. What is it?

If you cannot answer this question, I advise you to go back to when you were a child and ask yourself what you loved then. The problem is that as we get older, we eliminate many of our passions based on judgments of what we deem as practical or financially wise. We hear people telling us things like, "That's a hard field to get into!" "That will require a lot of hours!" "Not everyone succeeds in that business!" "You will be a starving artist!" and "That's not women's work (or men's work)!"

When we hear "practical" advice like this, we tend to shut down our inner knowing and no longer follow our vision and desires. This is because we want to be acceptable to others and care more about their approval than we do about connecting with our deeper self. While we may have abandoned ourselves on big decisions, like our careers, chances are we have abandoned ourselves on smaller decisions as well. Some examples might include where we want to live, what we want to wear, who we love, what we think about certain topics, what we want to do in our spare time and what we need emotionally.

Let's illustrate:
You had a vision when you were a kid, but everyone told you it was not practical.
You may be able to relate to this like Fred did, as well as my son-in-law, Charlie. Both were told their childhood dreams were impractical. Fred followed the path of his family business and did

not pursue his love of animals. Now he realizes he can create a pet-friendly work culture and allow pets and pet care at work. Charlie, a comedian, didn't listen to those who were critical of his career path and developed a comedic skit called *The Manitowoc Minute*—which went viral and earns him a very comfortable living. This goes to show it is never too late to pursue your vision and desires.

Where is it that you need to be true to yourself so that your passion can lead you to your purpose?

TODAY'S Affirmation:
"I am able to make choices in alignment with what I desire!"
-Susan K. Wehrley

ALIGN Challenge:
Look back to your younger years. What did you love doing? How might you re-kindle what you loved and make money doing it?

Day 4: Learn how to stay connected to your "why" so drama doesn't get you off track.

We are becoming fully aligned to our vision and desires when we develop a filter in our mind that sees only the possibilities of how to get there—not the obstacles.

When we hit an obstacle and our mind automatically asks, "How might I align to my vision and desires?"—we eliminate the drama that occurs, and we do the deeper work of discovering how to stay aligned to our vision, values and goals. Curiosity allows you to put the pieces of the puzzle together and see options you otherwise could not see.

Let's illustrate:
You have anxiety because you believe you have to constantly please everyone.
We know Rosemary struggles with this, and so might you at times! That is because her mind focused on what others wanted and how they might behave if she did not accommodate them. By shifting her orientation to her vision and desires—her "why"—she can think about possibilities to align her decisions accordingly. For example, Rosemary has a vision to have more quality time with her kids and herself so that she can be more present. Her "why" is that she believes connection creates happiness. So when her boss sends out that occasional email that says, "Who on the team can finish this project up tonight?" Rosemary can respond, "I could dedicate from 9-10 pm after the kids go to bed. Can anyone else also pitch in an hour? I think we could get it done then!"

You have anxiety because you often feel abandoned by others.
This is Fred's concern—he is never sure if his team will let him down or not! This triggers the deep abandonment issues he felt as a child when his dreams were never nurtured. Now that Fred understands he can only abandon himself, he approaches his team with much more clarity around "why" they need to have revenue

exceed the expenses. His vulnerability, along with his transparency of the numbers, helps his team support his vision and desires.

TODAY'S Affirmation:
"I am able to learn my lesson in life and help others as a result."
- Susan K. Wehrley

ALIGN Challenge:
How might you apply this to a situation you are currently facing?

Day 5: Don't get caught in the comparison trap that steals your passion.

When we compare ourselves to others, we lose our focus and our passion. It is an exhausting mindset, whether you come out on top or not. The sad thing is that the comparison trap makes us compete with others versus collaborate as we share our unique differences. The only way to break free from the comparison trap is to fully embrace who you are in your uniqueness—the good, the bad and the ugly.

When we don't embrace ourselves unconditionally and we compare ourselves to others, we go on a roller coaster ride of feeling self-doubt—to grandiosity. This is how the E.G.O. is formed (Edging our Greatest self Out), because we are wasting time comparing ourselves to others versus simply focusing on our passions so that we can reach our greatest potential.

All of us bring something valuable to this earth. When we focus on our passions, we expand our greatness. By embracing your unique personality traits, gifts, abilities, values, goals and desires, you can then aim for being more of who you were intended to be. When you covet your neighbor's life—personality, gifts, abilities or lifestyle—you lose focus on who you are as a unique person.

When we endlessly look at who others are and how they do things, we lose touch with what our inner guidance is telling us to do. When we look at the lives of others, we will always find something we lack. But when we look deeply into ourselves and listen to our passion, we get the guidance to become more of our greatest self. Nothing steals passion more than jealousy. Whether that passion is in a relationship or just passion for life, we feel passion when we embrace ourselves and love ourselves for exactly who we are. Only then can we be more excited, positive, brave and focused on becoming all we were intended to be.

Let's illustrate:
Someone posts their new dream house on Facebook—and you haven't bought yours yet.
Of course you compare! That is human. You feel disappointed that is not your life and perhaps feel less than—but hopefully for only a minute. OK, now you know what you are doing—so get over it! Do this by stopping the comparison trap. Instead, get curious and ask yourself, "What do I really want?" Be honest...do you want that dream house more than something else you are getting? Is there a way to get what you have AND your own dream house? Stop coveting and start exploring. Ask, "How might I be my best self and align to my vision, values and goals?"

TODAY'S Affirmation:
"I am able to appreciate others' lots in life, as well as my own."
- Susan K. Wehrley

ALIGN Challenge:
When in the past 30 days have you fallen into the comparison trap and it grabbed you, making you feel either less than or superior?

ALIGN Principle 8—ACCESS YOUR POWER

Days 1-5

Day 1: You are bigger than all that "stuff."

Now that you have the 8 Spiritual Principles, you know how to tap into your locus of control—your spirit-self. This is your power center to remind you how you're bigger than your circumstances and that there is something bigger than you to assist you. You know how to access possibilities to get you where you want to go. No person or circumstance can stop you.

Check in: Do you believe this?

This doesn't mean you are pushing to get where you want to go by perspired action. You know by now that this type of reaction is based in fear. You are bigger than all that "stuff" and realize you don't just bend with the wind. Your roots are deep, because you are connected with your inner source—your intuitive knowing that guides you through whatever comes your way.

You now have the mindset tools to create the results you want! Because you are in the present moment, you trust your Gut Intelligence to guide you as you make decisions. You are able to ALIGN to your vision, values and goals by accessing your inner power.

As Lao Tzu said, *"Mastering others is strength. Mastering yourself is true power."* The key to self-mastery is staying out of your own way. This means having a high level of personal awareness of how you sabotage the very vision and goals you say you want to achieve. Instead of allowing fear, self-doubt, double-minded thinking, limited-thinking and instant gratification to lead your life, you are instead able to root yourself in the ground and stand tall in your intention and convictions.

As Alice Walker said, *"The most common way people give up their power is by thinking they don't have any."* Change the way you think, and you will change your ability to have power over yourself and your world. This power comes from letting go of your fear that you will not get the outcome you want. You no longer wonder IF you will be safe, secure, loved and belong, you wonder HOW you will be safe, secure, loved and belong. Wondering HOW leads you into a connection with your intuitive self that will give you what you need in order to get what you want. This connection is your power source.

TODAY'S Affirmation:
"I am able to master my personal power by wondering "How," not "IF," I will get what I want."- Susan K. Wehrley

ALIGN Challenge:
Where do you need to have a mindset reset and wonder, "'HOW' might I get what I want?"

Day 2: Lead yourself to a connection with your power.

Accessing your power means you are rooted in your connection with your intuitive guidance within. This means you are not a tree that blows in the wind. You have roots that go deep into the ground like an oak tree that knows you are strong and unmovable. Your roots come from your ability to make a deep connection with yourself. When things are not going as you hoped, instead of looking outside yourself for validation and strength, you spend more quiet time listening to that inner guidance within.

You do this because you understand no one else knows the right solution or direction for you. This is a very personal journey, and you trust yourself to be able to connect with your power, which is your wisdom within that is ready to guide you.

While others may believe they do not have time to slow their lives down to get quiet, you know you need to quiet your mind. Quieting your mind is the first step to accessing your power. Once you quiet your mind, you ask your intuition to give you guidance. You do this by asking one good question at a time, then listening deeply within. You know the power question you need to ask: **"How might I...?"**

When you ask this one simple question, breathe deeply and quiet your mind, you access your subconscious mind to put the pieces of the puzzle together for you. Your subconscious mind has been picking up the cues all along. You just needed to quiet your mind to access your subconscious power so that it could go to work for you. This is an act of surrender to something bigger than you at work.

As a result of this personal power practice, you become clear on what you need to do or say. You know it is your intuitive mind at work, because you suddenly get this "a-ha" knowing—a heightened awareness that gives you chills all over your body and says, "That's it!" Now you are clear, calm and confident on what you need to do or say.

It is this clarity and connection within that makes you feel so powerful. When you are not clear and deeply connected to yourself, you are like a fragile tree blowing in the wind. In contrast, when you get clear and connected deeply within yourself, you get the confidence to do what you need to do. No longer are you focused on the future and what outcomes may or may not happen. Instead, you are in the present moment and aware of what you need to do. You are open, you trust intuition, and you allow it to show you through the maze of possibilities.

TODAY'S Affirmation:
*"I am able to access my power with one simple question:
"How might I...?"*- Susan K. Wehrley

ALIGN Challenge:
Looking back at the last 30 days, where could you have accessed your power before taking action?

Day 3: Be unafraid in the face of adversity and criticism.

Adversity is what tests our true power. While we may naturally dislike adversity, we have a choice to see it differently. Adversity can be the biggest catalyst to accessing our power and aligning us to our best self. Everyone faces adversity from time to time. What matters is how we deal with it. When we cultivate the inner wisdom to overcome adversity, we develop our personal power.

Walt Disney said, "All the adversity I've had in my life, all the troubles and obstacles, have strengthened me. You may not realize it when it happens, but a kick in the teeth may be the best thing in the world for you." William Shakespeare referred to adversity this way, "Let me embrace thee, sour adversity, for wise men say it is the wisest course."

While adversity may not be fun, it can be the catalyst to build our wisdom. Our wisdom is our power. When we put our wisdom to use and execute what we know we need to do or say, instead of wimping out, we develop our power.

Criticism, like adversity, can challenge our power. We find our power when we choose to follow our inner wisdom instead of being afraid if we are right or wrong, good or bad. It is much easier to conform to the norms of others than it is to find our power amidst group-think. Instead of claiming our truth and authenticity, many will choose to forego expressing or even knowing what their wisdom is telling them. This is because they are choosing safety, security, love and belonging over wisdom and inner strength. However, once we have built this tether to our inner wisdom, we no longer feel compelled to abandon ourselves for the approval of others.

Let's illustrate:
You are unhappy with your family dynamics.
You decide to be bold and confront the person you believe is

causing family discord. You do this first with curiosity, and you don't approach them with judgment. However, you also speak your truth—sharing how their behavior affects you and makes you feel as well as the vision and desire you have for the relationship. Because you are tethered to your inner power, you can hear their point of view and consider what they are saying no matter how they react or respond. This power allows you to speak your truth, listen, honor others' truth and needs, and then choose boundaries accordingly.

TODAY'S Affirmation:
"I am able to face adversity and criticism when I listen to my wisdom and not the criticism of others."- Susan K. Wehrley

ALIGN Challenge:
Looking back at the last 30 days, where could you have been more true to yourself and in your power?

Day 4: Stay firm and true to yourself.

Most people find it difficult to stay firm and true to themselves. They get unconsciously attached to the outcome of their basic human needs—safety, security, love and belonging.

Abandoning our true self and power is as simple as:
- Biting our tongues.
- Being afraid to speak up.
- Living in denial.
- Pretending we are sweet when we really are angry.
- Avoiding conflict because we prefer the instant gratification of peace in the moment with others versus the inner peace that comes from us being true to ourselves.
- Accommodating others' expectations instead of being true to ourselves and letting go of their reaction or judgment .

Abandoning oneself is more common than being true to oneself. That's why as you become more powerful, others will often feel intimidated by you. Instead of them owning their insecurity and seeing you as a role model, they will see you as a light to their darkness. Instead of being vulnerable about how your strength makes them feel insecure, many will project their fear onto you with hateful, spiteful or negative opinions of you. I call this "switch and blame"—a technique to get the heat off of them and back onto you. Being powerful means: You see their negative remarks for exactly what they are—fear and insecurity.

Because you are powerful, you do not have to cave into their shaming remarks. Knowing who you are is part of your power. However, this isn't to say you can't learn from positive and constructive feedback and improve yourself. But when someone is doing a "switch and blame," you will know it! It's a defense mechanism so they do not have to look at themselves.

In order to stay firm and true to yourself, surround yourself with people who get you and support you. Choose your friends and "family" wisely. Better to be alone than to be with people who do not give you love and honor you for who you truly are. Most importantly, treat yourself kindly. In order to stay true to yourself and treat yourself kindly, you must love yourself unconditionally. This means that you know you have work to do on reaching your greatest potential—but in the meantime, you feel good about yourself. Every flaw you have makes you who you are, and you know you can one day grow into your best purpose.

TODAY'S Affirmation:
"I am able to stay firm and true to myself, no matter what others think of me."
- *Susan K. Wehrley*

ALIGN Challenge:
Looking back at the last 30 days, where could you have stayed firmer and truer to yourself?

Day 5: Keep a level head of self-assurance.

One of the greatest ways to keep a level head of self-assurance is to stay present in the moment. We can do this by using a mind mantra that will neutralize our emotions:

> *"It is what it is...now the question becomes, 'How might I deal with this present moment?'"*

When we first square with the reality of a situation and then wonder how to be with it, we become self-assured. This self-assurance comes to us because we snap out of over-thinking, trust our Gut Intelligence, and do whatever it is we need to do. Because you are not fighting the reality of what is, you get in the flow of what is meant to be. To keep a level head of self-assurance in difficult situations, ask yourself:

> *"How might I deal with this present moment?"*

Self-assured people understand that you must stop to lighten up if you want to tap into your self-assurance. By lightening up, we become more self-assured that our thoughts and emotions are not who we are or the predictor of outcomes. We just observe our thoughts and emotions and then shift out of them into our possibility-thinking. By lightening up, we lighten our grip on our attachments to certain outcomes of safety, security, love and belonging.

By lightening up, you can more easily shift back into your level head of self-assurance. Realizing there is abundance around you when something doesn't go exactly as you had hoped, you say to yourself:

> *"OK...that was disappointing...but this or something better is coming my way!!!"*

The self-assured person understands there is not just one way to the outcome they want—there are many possibilities. By being open-minded and in the present moment, you will become self-assured.

Let's illustrate:
You were hoping to see someone you love over the holidays, but they chose other plans.
To stay in your power, you can say to yourself, "OK...that was disappointing...but, how might I make this the best holiday ever without them so that I can enjoy the present moment?"

TODAY'S Affirmation:
"I am able to shift out of my E.G.O. and become self-assured that all is for my highest good."
- Susan K. Wehrley

ALIGN Challenge:
Looking back at the last 30 days, when did you get stuck, instead of shifting to your self-assurance?

SECTION IV

Self-Assessment

One of the best ways to align to your best self as you achieve your vision, values and goals, is to get honest about how you are getting in your own way. Take these two assessments, which will help you realize what you need to focus on so that you can realize your full potential!

Increased Gut Intelligence allows us to achieve Intuitive Alignment. But do you stay aligned to your spirit-self when you are facing people and situations that trigger your fear? Practicing the 8 Spiritual Principles helps us to maintain the level of Intuitive Alignment, the highest form of Gut Intelligence, more often. When we are at the level of Intuitive Alignment, we are our best selves as we align to our vision, values and goals.

Take the mini self-assessments below to help you focus on a plan for reaching your full potential!

Gut Intelligence Assessment
How often do you find yourself in each level of Gut Intelligence, considering the varying aspects of your life? Rate yourself at each level and be honest. Rate: 1-Never; 2-Sometimes; 3-Average; 4-Mostly; 5-Always

___**Level 1: Unawareness** is a state of unconsciousness where we often do not feel the ping in our gut that alerts us. As a result, we often go into an unconscious fight or flight behavior to deal with people or situations. This state of unawareness causes a lot of drama in our lives, instead of reflection and discernment on how we could otherwise align to our vision, values and goals.

___**Level 2: Judgment and Self-doubt** is a state of awareness where we are realizing our pain, but we believe others are causing it or somehow it was our fault. As a result, there is a lot of projection onto others, believing they need to change for our unhappiness—or we waste energy self-loathing. While we feel the gut alert and know what is occurring is not in alignment with our heart desires, we don't do anything to make the situation better.

___**Level 3: Self-Awareness** means you become aware of what's not working in your life, what triggers you, and how your E.G.O. steps in to react or take control. By noticing your own personal patterns of reaction, you can detach from your need to take things personally or your tendency to want to control the outcome. To remain at this level of awareness, it's important to make this self-observation without self-judgment.

___**Level 4: Detachment** allows you to see more clearly how your need and attachment for safety, security, love and belonging are causing you pain. By observing your fears that you may not get what you want, you can detach from your stronghold and simply observe what is happening. This frees you to get a curious attitude that asks, "How might I make the most of this situation and align to my vision, values and goals?" Now you are detached and in a problem-solving mindset so you can begin to create the life you want.

___**Level 5: Intuitive Alignment** occurs when we stay open-minded and ask a curious, "How might I (or we)...?" question. By asking our intuition for guidance and then letting go of control, we align to the spirit-voice within rather than our E.G.O. voice. Because we no longer have the need to be right or in control, we can surrender to this spirit-within for guidance without fear or attachment to the outcome. As a result, we become more clear, calm and confident in our decision-making.

Personal Reflection:
At which level do you primarily operate?

What do you need to do to get to Level 5: Intuitive Alignment?

Increasing your Gut Intelligence, and staying at Level 5: Intuitive Alignment, requires practice of the 8 Spiritual Principles. This is especially true when we face situations and people that normally cause us stress. Stress triggers lead to a tendency to react, instead of respond, which can send us back into the lower levels of Gut Intelligence.

8 Spiritual Principles Assessment
How well do you practice the 8 Spiritual Principles, especially when you are facing difficult people and situations? Rate yourself at each level and be honest.
Rate: 1-Never; 2-Sometimes; 3-Average; 4-Mostly; 5-Always

___**Principle 1—BE HUMBLE:** To be humble means to realize we don't always have to have the answer. This means we develop a modest estimation of our own individual importance and begin to realize it is something bigger than ourselves that is in control. Being humble is giving up the ego's need for self-importance, control and being right.

___**Principle 2—ASK, BELIEVE AND RECEIVE:** This means we ask our spirit-self, however we define that relationship, for guidance to help us along the way. This entails opening our mindset, believing what you want exists, and drawing it to you. This means eliminating the "wishing" and "yearning" that tells the subconscious mind, "What you want does not exist!" That was the limited, double-minded and self-deprecating thinking that held you back!

___**Principle 3—FORGIVE, LET GO AND LEARN:** By quickly forgiving ourselves for being attached again to our E.G.O.'s perceptions and needs, and therefore our reactions, we can let go and be in the present moment, experiencing all we are intended to experience—including what we are intended to learn. This principle applies to us and others we encounter who are also here to grow and learn.

___**Principle 4—STAY OPEN-MINDED AND GET CURIOUS:** Staying open-minded allows us to get curious about why we are experiencing what we are, why we are getting what we want, how others think differently, etc. Being open-minded and curious connects us more deeply to our intuitive self and to others. This principle teaches us to be without fear as we observe life's unfoldment.

___**Principle 5—PRACTICE GRATITUDE:** Gratitude helps us to not waste time or thoughts of disappointment and frustration on things we can't control. Because we have developed the quality of being grateful, we have a readiness to receive more abundance. This allows us to master our mind: What we think about, we bring about—and what we focus on expands.

___**Principle 6—EMBRACE GRACE AND SYNCRONICITY:** As you master Principle 6, you heighten your awareness that "all is perfect!" As a result of this belief, you acknowledge that grace and synchronicity are in your life to assist you! The path of success becomes lighter and less burdened because of this shift in mindset.

___**Principle 7—FOCUS ON YOUR VISION AND DESIRE:** Instead of focusing on what others should be doing, who they should be, or what you deem should be happening to you—you spend your energy on being curious, like, "How might I reach my own vision, values and goals?" Instead of worrying about how things are unfolding and when and how you will get there, you stay in the present moment and feel how great it will feel when you arrive!

___**Principle 8: ACCESS YOUR POWER:** Now you understand the power in surrendering and abiding in your spirit-self instead of your ego-self. You do this by automatically asking for guidance with a question that begins with, "How might I (we)...?" Instead of working hard on your own power, you work smart—by regularly listening to and aligning with the power within.

Personal Reflection:
What principles do you need to focus on most?

Why?

As a result of aligning to your greatest potential, Level 5: Intuitive Alignment, you are now able to live a life of more happiness and love. You understand that people who live with more happiness and love don't necessarily have more perfect lives. What they do have is an ability to be clear, calm and confident during what may appear as imperfect times.

When their basic needs of safety security, love and belonging are threatened, they are aware of what is causing the fearful chattering in their mind and own whatever attachment is showing up for them to heal: safety, security, love or belonging. By acknowledging their state of mind, owning it, breathing through the anxiety, and letting go of the thoughts causing their fear, they return to a life of love and happiness. This creates a freedom and independence from the inner mindset disturbances that once stole their peace, happiness and feelings of love.

Summary Discussion:
1) Which level would you currently say you are in?
   ___Level 1: Unawareness
   ___Level 2: Judgment and Self-doubt
   ___Level 3: Self-awareness
   ___Level 4: Detachment
   ___Level 5: Intuitive Alignment

2) What attachments do you need to let go of: safety, security, love or belonging?

3) What situations are most difficult for you to detach from? Why?

4) How will detaching help you get to Level 5: Intuitive Alignment?

5) What will the benefits be for you to continually work towards Level 5: Intuitive Alignment?

6) What is your action plan to solidify your development towards Level 5: Intuitive Alignment?

7) How well have you mastered the 8 Principles?
   Rate: 1-Never; 2-Sometimes; 3-Average; 4-Mostly; 5-Always
   ___Be Humble
   ___Ask, Believe, and Receive
   ___Forgive, Let Go and Learn

___Stay Open-minded and Trust Your Gut
___Practice Gratitude
___Embrace Grace and Synchronicity
___Focus on Your Vision and Desire
___Access Your Power

8) What is your vision for your life?

9) What are your values?

10) What are your goals?

Use the Action Sheet in the book to chart out your plan.
Remember: While a plan helps us focus, using our Gut Intelligence keeps us aligned in those everyday moments of truth! God Bless!

SUSAN K. WEHRLEY'S BOOKS

Check out Susan's books for more information on how you can become more clear, calm and confident:

Gut Intelligence: ALIGN

Gut Intelligence

EGO at Work

Ignite the Plan

PAUSE

Personal Leadership Puzzle

The Power to Believe

The Secret to "I AM"

You can learn more at: www.BIZremedies.com

www.ingramcontent.com/pod-product-compliance
Lightning Source LLC
Chambersburg PA
CBHW061256110426
42742CB00012BA/1939